With Hope in Your Heart

With Hope in Your Heart

THE SEÁN COX STORY

MARTINA COX

with Susan Keogh

Gill Books

Gill Books
Hume Avenue
Park West
Dublin 12
www.gillbooks.ie

Gill Books is an imprint of M.H. Gill and Co.

© Martina Cox 2020
978 07171 9010 2

Print origination by O'K Graphic Design
Copy-edited by Susan McKeever
Proofread by Emma Dunne
Printed by CPI Group (UK) Ltd, Croydon, CRO 4YY

This book is typeset in 13.5/18 pt Minion.

The paper used in this book comes from the wood pulp of managed forests. For every tree felled, at least one tree is planted, thereby renewing natural resources.

A CIP catalogue record for this book is available from the British Library.

5 4 3 2 1

About the Authors

Seán and Martina Cox have three children and live in Dunboyne, Co. Meath. While Seán requires full-time medical care, is not likely to walk again and finds speech and many other daily tasks challenging, his family are determined to give him the best treatments available to ensure he can live as normal a life as possible.

Susan Keogh is a journalist who has been working in Irish media for the last 16 years. She currently presents *Newstalk Breakfast* on Saturday and Sunday mornings.

FOREWORD

Seán Cox. In one way, I wish that I had never heard this name. If I hadn't, it would mean that he had come to our match against A.S. Roma on the night of 24 April 2018, enjoyed a wonderful game and gone home safely to his family to tell them all the stories of an unforgettable occasion.

All of our other supporters who were at Anfield that night were able to do this. It is why we fall in love with football – the passion, the drama, the joy, the pleasure. We live the moment and then we get to share the moment with others, especially during special times for whichever team we support.

Seán never got to do this and this is something that hurt the players and myself a great deal at the time. He is and always will be one of our own, and learning that he had become a victim of what I would describe as the ugly side of football had a big effect on everyone in the Liverpool family.

The way that family then pulled together, though, showed football and society at its best. I always say that football is the most important of the least important things, but this kind of solidarity takes it to a different level.

In this respect, I feel privileged to know the name Seán Cox. In his fight, in how his family dealt with a terrible situation and in the way people came together he represents everything that is good about Liverpool Football Club.

I also feel blessed to have been able to meet Seán and his family. Seeing him in person was something that I feared may never happen, so when it did the experience moved the players and myself more than you can imagine.

We have been fortunate to enjoy some special moments at the club recently, but seeing Seán at Anfield was definitely one of the high points for all of us. Just knowing he would be at the stadium was important for all of the team and we hope he will be able to return to Anfield in the future.

Having been fortunate enough to spend some time with Seán and his family, I can say without any doubt that this book is a love story. Their love and devotion has been clear from the very first day that I was told they had travelled to Liverpool from Ireland to be at his bedside.

I often get asked about leadership in football, but in 'real life' I can think of no greater example of what a leader is than Seán's wife, Martina. I cannot claim to know her well, but I have followed what she has done for her husband and her family and it has humbled me.

Like everyone else, I would give anything to change what happened to Seán, but at the same time I feel honoured to have encountered such a special individual and his incredible family.

He and they will never walk alone.

Jürgen Klopp
Liverpool, July 2020

CONTENTS

NOW

PROLOGUE

I place my mobile phone back down on the kitchen island and stare at it. I feel nothing. Numb. Paralysed. I can't move. What did she just say? 'Seán has been injured.' I repeat the four words, but they still make no sense to me. What did she mean? 'Seán has been injured.' It was like she'd been speaking a different language. I look back at my phone. Had I just imagined the call? Seán wasn't injured; I saw him this morning. He had sent me a text message a few hours ago.

'He's in an ambulance on his way to hospital.' What had she been talking about? The words swirl around my brain. Seán is in Liverpool. He's been there hundreds of times. He is at the match. He's safe. He's not injured. He's not in an ambulance. I picture him standing at my side of the bed that morning. He kissed me goodbye and told me he'd check in with me later. As I rolled over, he walked out the bedroom door with his little overnight bag on his back. I closed my eyes and went back to sleep. Was this a nightmare?

Suddenly I am aware of the sound of the television. It's coming from the living room where Jack is eating his dinner.

He has just come back from GAA training to watch the Liverpool match. The match his dad was at.

I go from feeling nothing to everything. I need to know more. Or do I? What if knowing is worse than not knowing? I look back at my phone, lying on the kitchen island like a weapon. I want to throw it against the wall. I want to watch it break into a hundred pieces and fall to the ground. I want it to never again tell me things I don't want to hear. I should have gone running this evening. Why didn't I go? I always went running on a Tuesday night. What had stopped me? I thought about my feet pounding the ground beneath me. The simple task of putting one foot in front of another. The joy of always moving forward. Slow and steady with the wind in my hair. My mind calmer with each stride until eventually there's nothing. Complete freedom. I should have gone running. I could have just kept running, away from all of this.

I stand up and start to pace. Up and down the kitchen. I had been thinking about Christmas all day: little red velvet dresses, Santa pyjamas for boys and girls, Rudolf babygrows. For most people Christmas is still eight months away, but in the retail world plans are in full swing.

What will I tell the kids? I wonder as Shauna walks into the kitchen. How do I explain something I don't understand myself? I do my best. I stay calm on the outside, but inside I'm panicking. They can't process it either and join me in pacing up and down the kitchen as we wait for something to happen. We all agree it can't be true. There must have been a mistake. Some sort of breakdown in communication. They've got the wrong man. It's not Seán. My husband. Their dad. This news was destined for some other poor family but got lost along the way. This news doesn't belong to us. We clutch at straws. 'If Dad is injured, it can't be serious. He probably just needs a few stitches,' says Jack. We agree.

Seán's brother Peter arrives. We pump him for information, but nobody really knows what's happened. Emma! Where's Emma? Our youngest is on her way home from Irish dancing. I make my way to the door to meet her. I must tell her not to worry, that everything is okay. I cry when I see her. Back in the kitchen it's harder to pace. The house has started to fill up. Family, friends and neighbours. Everyone wants to help. No one knows what to say.

My mobile rings. I freeze. I should have smashed it, I think. My eyes fall on the screen and I recognise an English number. I grab the phone.

'Hello,' I say nervously.

'Is this Martina Cox?' asks the woman on the other end. I hold my breath as she tells me she is a nurse at Aintree University Hospital. 'Seán was attacked outside Anfield. I looked after him when he arrived here by ambulance,' she tells me calmly.

I open my mouth, but nothing comes out.

'Your husband has a bleed on the brain, Martina. We've transferred him to a neurological hospital for surgery.'

All I can feel is fear. My hands start to shake, and I concentrate hard on not dropping my phone. I push it to my ear to hear her better. I open my mouth again. I don't know what I'm going to say until I say it.

'Is he dead?' I scream.

BEFORE

When You Know,
You Know

'Seán, this is Martina, from work,' said Suzanne Cox to her brother. I was standing at the door of the living room in their family home in Clondalkin in Dublin. The noise of a football match blared from the TV sitting in the corner, filling the room. He took his eyes off the action for a moment to turn and wave. 'Hello,' I said shyly. I worked with Suzanne in Dunnes Stores in Kilnamanagh and we had become good friends. We knew a lot of the same people and enjoyed nights out together. I was only 20 years old and I had just broken up with my very first boyfriend. We had been going out for about a year but now I was single, and Suzanne was determined to set me up with Seán. 'You're both the same age, and he's lovely – what have you got to lose?' she coaxed.

A few weeks later she brought him along on a night out. With no football to distract him, the second introduction went better, and he asked me out for a drink. The following week we met in his local pub, The Steering Wheel in Clondalkin. We clicked straight away. Seán had also recently broken up with someone. But that wasn't the only thing we had in common. Before long the conversation started to flow. I lived not too far away in Walkinstown, so we knew a lot of the same people. We were both quite shy, but immediately we felt comfortable in each other's company. He came across as a very kind person, and sensible too, but with a glint in his eye. He also had a great sense of humour and made me laugh without even trying. My 21st birthday was coming up and I had planned a party in the function room of the Red Cow Hotel in Dublin. I was really looking forward to it, and I asked Seán to come along. My ex-boyfriend was also there on the night. I felt obliged to ask him – we'd only recently broken up and there were no hard feelings between us. 'You didn't tell me he was going to be here,' Seán said as soon as he realised. It didn't really bother him, though, and we laughed it off. I think we both knew this was different. It sounds like such a cliché but even back then I felt that Seán was 'the one'. He was gentle and thoughtful, and the type of person who would do anything for you.

He used to wear these awful sleeveless slipover jumpers and I remember after a couple of weeks I said to him, 'Seán, you're going to have to lose those jumpers if we're going to go the distance.' Seán's two brothers, Peter and Marty, were constantly teasing him over his dress sense. 'Where are ya going in that jumper?' they'd say to him, laughing. Even years later when Seán went shopping, he found it difficult to put an outfit together. He'd go into the shop and find a mannequin he liked the look of; he'd then study each piece of clothing, figuring out how the whole look was put together before setting about buying every item. Seán was never one to be defeated. In those early days when we first got together, we didn't have a whole lot of money, but Seán always tried to bring me places or treat me to things he knew I liked. He was sweet. We enjoyed going to the movies and going out for a drink whenever we could. We also spent a lot of time in each other's houses. The baby of Seán's family, Sinéad, was only 10 at the time, so we used to babysit her every Thursday night when his parents went out for a drink. Getting to and from each other's houses wasn't easy in those days as there were no buses running from Clondalkin where Seán lived to my house in Walkinstown. It never stopped Seán, though. He used to walk to see me. I laugh when I remember that time, it was such a long walk, but there was no other way. The quickest route involved Seán taking a shortcut through an industrial estate. I remember one night as he made his way home, he was nearly attacked by a group of angry Alsatian dogs. They had been guarding a premises but had broken free. They ran for Seán, who managed to get himself to safety by climbing up onto a high gate. He had to stay there until the dogs got bored with him. He rang me the next day to fill me in. 'I'm never walking down to you again!' he threatened. But it wasn't long before he changed his mind. He never turned up on a Wednesday evening, though, always making up some excuse for his absence. It never bothered me but years later it dawned on me that it was his other love that kept him away: sport. There was always football on the television on a Wednesday night and he just couldn't miss it. Seán's deep love of sport, in particular GAA and Liverpool Football Club, is something that has been a huge part of our lives. He would literally watch two flies climbing up the wall. The type of sport was irrelevant – he was interested in golf and Gaelic, snooker and soccer, rugby and darts. He was constantly channel-hopping, looking for whatever bit of action was on offer. An absolute sports fanatic.

Our relationship progressed from those early days very quickly; I think that was just the way it was back then. If you met someone and fell in love, everything else just fell into place. It was straightforward, and it certainly went that way for us. Seán's sister Suzanne had also started going out with a guy named Seán, who was from Galway but worked with us in Dunnes Stores. We all got on really well and socialised a lot together in those early years. One of our regular haunts was Flamingo's nightclub in Stillorgan. It was the place to be in Dublin at the time. I still remember the excitement of a big night out, getting dressed up and meeting friends before joining the long queue outside. It was always a relief to get past the bouncers and make your way inside. The latest tunes filled the air as we danced the night away, the mirror balls glistening above our heads. We always went home smelling of cigarette smoke and beer, but it didn't matter. Everyone had fun and that was the most important thing. One particular weekend, a year after myself and Seán met, we made our way out for what I expected was going to be another regular night at Flamingos. But Seán had other plans. As the lights dimmed and the DJ announced it was time for the slow set, Seán grabbed my hand. 'Let's go,' he said, smiling. Other couples emerged from different corners of the nightclub and walked towards the dance floor. In those days the slow set was the big moment of the night. We followed the crowd through and found a place to dance. And then as the familiar beats of one of Seán's favourite songs, 'I Want to Know What

Love Is', began, he asked me to marry him. It might sound like an odd thing to say but I wasn't surprised. The proposal that particular night took me by surprise – I had no idea he planned to do it there and then – but I knew very early on we'd spend the rest of our lives together. 'Yes,' I answered, with the biggest smile on my face. It was that simple. They say, 'when you know you know', and that was most definitely the case with me and Seán. I remember getting home to my parents' house that night. I was so excited. I really wanted to wake them up and tell them, but it was late, so I went to bed. The next morning, I filled them in on everything that had happened. I was worried they'd think it was too soon, we were only going out a year, but they already knew it was the real deal. They had seen how happy we were together.

A few days later we went to buy the ring. 'There was no way I was going to pick the right one,' said Seán. He wanted us to choose it together. 'You have to love it; you'll be wearing it forever,' he said. We decided to get married the following year and spent the next 12 months working and saving. We bought a little red car, a Fiat 127, and we were so thrilled with ourselves, you'd think we had bought a BMW. We got into a rhythm and life was simple and straightforward. We both worked in Dublin city centre. Seán was with an electrical company called GEC which was based on Hendrick Street and I was working in Dunnes Stores on George's Street. Every morning Seán picked me up at home and we'd drive into town to work together. Afterwards he'd collect me and drive me home. Before our wedding the following year, we brought my parents, Paddy and Ann Bannon, to meet Seán's parents, Martin and Yvonne Cox, for the first time at the

Green Isle Hotel in Dublin. Everyone got on well, which was down in no small part to the fact that both of our families were quite similar. We were cut from the same cloth. We were all set.

On 8 July 1989, at the age of 23, I was walked by my dad up the aisle of the Church of the Holy Spirit in Greenhills to marry Seán. I was wearing a satin dress that I had gotten a dressmaker to make for me after I came across the material and fell in love with it. My sisters, Catherine and Bernie, were my bridesmaids and Seán's little sister, Sinéad, was my flower girl. Seán looked so smart when I met him at the altar, suited and booted in his traditional morning dress of black jacket and grey pinstripe trousers. I remember someone telling me afterwards that he had forgotten to take the price tag off the sole of his new shoes so when he knelt down everyone could see it. I laughed. 'Typical Seán,' I said to myself. Our families and friends surrounded us in love as we took our wedding vows. 'To have and to hold from this day forward, for better, for worse, for richer, for poorer, in sickness and in health.' We pulled out all the stops and partied the night away at the Kilternan Hotel in Dublin. 'I Want to Know What Love Is' filled the room as we took to the dance floor for our first dance. It couldn't be any other song.

We chose Cyprus for our honeymoon and booked the most wonderful hotel. When we were leaving, we decided to take two glasses with us from the hotel as a souvenir. We packed them in our cases and headed for the airport to make our way home. When we got there, we were shocked to find that the police were checking people's bags. Both of us had only been outside of Ireland once before so we panicked, thinking we were going to get in trouble for taking the glasses. I went into the ladies' toilets and Seán went into the gents' and we unpacked the glasses from our cases and left them there. When I think back on that now it reminds me how young and naive we were. We were only in our early twenties; we were both babies. The police were definitely not there to apprehend people with souvenir glasses in their bags! We boarded our flight for Dublin ready to start our new life together. Little did we know that our first year of marriage was going to take away a lot of that innocence. More than our fair share of sadness was about to arrive at our door.

1989

The Cox family is the definition of a tightly knit unit. Seán's mam, Yvonne was a brilliant woman and a very dedicated mother. She was the glue that held all seven of them together. Seán was born in April 1965, the same year as me, and is the second oldest of five, two brothers, Peter and Marty, and two sisters, Suzanne and Sinéad. Seán's love of sport began when he was a baby – before he was even out of nappies – and that was down to one man, his dad. Martin Cox senior was GAA mad. He was originally from Boyle in Roscommon but despite settling down in Clondalkin in Dublin he supported Roscommon his whole life. And he brought his three sons along with him. Any time Roscommon had a match, no matter where it was in the country, Martin senior would put the three boys in the back of the car and all four of them would travel to cheer the team on. They never missed a match and over the years they travelled the length and breadth of the country to show their support. Seán inherited his dad's love for the GAA and as a child he played with Round Towers in Clondalkin. He loved it, the game, the camaraderie with his teammates, the craic, the sense of community at the heart of the club. At 18 Seán broke his arm and the injury forced him off the pitch, but he was determined to stay involved with the club. He didn't want to miss out so he set about finding another way to get his GAA fix. 'I'll be a manager,' he decided.

And that's what he did: he started to manage a younger team. It wasn't ever an option to not be involved with the club – it was in his DNA. In fact, sport in general was the heartbeat of Seán's childhood. When it came to soccer, however, they weren't all cheering for the same team. Martin senior was a Manchester United supporter, Seán and Marty were (and still are) avid Liverpool fans while Arsenal is Peter's team. The rivalry and slagging that went on in their childhood home was off the charts. Poor Peter had to fight the hardest for some space on the walls of the bedroom the three of them shared for his Arsenal heroes. Three of the four walls were covered with the faces of Liverpool legends Kenny Dalglish, Phil Thompson, Graeme Souness and Ian Rush. Regardless of the weather, endless hours were spent in the back garden kicking a football around as all three of them tried to recreate the skills of their idols. Their passion for soccer never waned as the years went by, and neither did the rivalry. Seán remembered his childhood very fondly – he was so close to his mam and dad and to his four siblings. When they were young they holidayed religiously in Sligo. Martin senior was adamant he would never set foot on a plane, so three times a year they booked a stay at Ryan's Hotel in Rosses Point, which is now the Yeats Country Hotel. They went every Easter, during the summer months and for the October Bank Holiday weekend. They even stayed in the same room, number 106. Seán often remarked how gas this was as it was also the number of the house they grew up in in Clondalkin. As a family they had the best of times together and Seán definitely inherited his love of tradition and routine from his parents. Seán and his siblings also spent a lot of time with their cousins when they were younger, in particular the Smith family. Seán's mam, Yvonne, had just one brother, Ken Smith, who she was very close to. Ken was married to Renee and they had five children, Richard, Barry, Raymond, Stephen and Alison. Over the years the five Cox children and the five Smith children were thrown together at every birthday party, Christmas and whatever family occasion was being celebrated at the time. Seán and Richard got on particularly well; they were closest in age and also had a lot of similar interests. It wasn't long after I started going out with Seán that I was introduced to Richard and his girlfriend, Una. We all got on like a house on fire so we started to meet up a lot, and do things together as a foursome.

After arriving home from honeymoon we settled into married life. We had bought a bungalow in Clondalkin from my sister Bernie and we were both back working hard after what had been a summer to remember. But by the time October came it felt like things around us were really starting to unravel. Richard's younger brother Stephen had been sick for a while. He was only 18 years of age and had been diagnosed with leukemia. He was such a lovely boy, too young to be sick. 'He's young – he'll fight it,' everyone said at the time. And he tried so hard. A few months before our wedding he had undergone a bone marrow transplant at St James's Hospital in Dublin, but sadly it didn't work. I remember Ken and Renee and Richard and Una leaving our wedding reception early to catch a flight to the UK. They were going to meet a consultant to discuss whether a second bone marrow transplant should be carried out. They wanted to do everything in their power to give Stephen the best chance of surviving. A decision was made to carry out a second transplant, so Richard donated bone marrow to Stephen for a second time. He would have done anything to save his little brother. But sadly the second attempt also failed and Stephen passed away in October 1989. Ken and Renee were devastated by the cruelty of one of their babies going before them. The whole family felt heartbroken over the loss of such a young life. Then four weeks later the unimaginable happened. Ken Smith had a heart attack and died. He was just 49 years of age. It was devastating. Renee had only just buried her son and now, one month later, her husband was dead. Everyone was so shocked that something like this could happen again. It was so hard on Richard, Barry, Raymond and Alison to lose their brother and then their dad. Seán's mam, Yvonne also really felt the loss of her only brother.

Then on 11 December, the following month, I got a phone call at work that would change the rest of our lives. At this stage I was working at the head office of Dunnes Stores. It was Seán. 'Dad's been in a road accident and he's dead,' he said. I couldn't believe my ears; I just didn't know what to think. Seán had been told to go to Kildare where the crash happened, and he was going. 'Don't go by yourself,' I begged him. I really wanted someone to go with him but he didn't have time for that so off he went, alone. If someone needed Seán, he answered their call: that was just the way he was. Seán's mam was at home in Clondalkin. I left work and made my way to her house in a total daze. When I got there, I learned that Martin Cox senior had been on his way to work in Naas in Co. Kildare in his van when a truck jackknifed and crashed into him, killing him instantly. Martin owned a business that made office partitions. Seán identified his dad's body, an experience that would give him nightmares for years. It hit him really hard. How much heartache could one family take? Three untimely deaths. Three funerals. In only three months. My heart was broken for all of them. There was so much sadness and worry around at that time. Our happy wedding celebration just three months before seemed like it had happened in a different lifetime. But Seán's family did what most Irish families do when their backs are to the wall: they pulled together and minded one another. They didn't have much choice. Three of the children were still at home with Yvonne, including the youngest, Sinéad, who was only 11 the time. She hadn't even made her Confirmation and now her dad was dead. As was the case with many families in eighties Ireland, Yvonne was a stay-at-home mam and Martin senior the breadwinner. They were devastated at his loss – they knew how much he'd be missed in the family home. But there was also going to be a lot of financial strain on the family, so everyone pulled together to do whatever they could.

Seán had been working in his local pub, The Steering Wheel in Clondalkin, since he was old enough to get a job. 'The responsible and organised type' was how his brothers described him. I think they looked up to him because he seemed to know where he was going in life. According to Marty and Peter, when Seán was younger he had a plan: get a job, meet a girl, get married, buy a house and have children. I remember the very first day I met Seán's brother Marty. We had been walking through Clondalkin village holding hands when Marty came around the corner. 'Well now, who is this?' he said to Seán with a big smile on his face. He knew Seán's plan was coming together. When Martin senior died so suddenly and tragically, Seán took on the role of father figure in the house. He was the eldest boy so it was just the thing to do. Yvonne became our priority. It came naturally to Seán to do whatever he could for her. Seán has always been a go-to person for people, a listening ear. He was always on hand to hear a problem and offer whatever advice he could. In the years after Seán's dad passed away we continued the family tradition of going to Sligo for years. We took Yvonne and our own children to Ryans Hotel every New Year's Eve, often joined by Seán's siblings and their families. It always felt like a fitting tribute to Martin senior. Sinéad, the baby of the family, grew up and met Ross and when they got married Seán took on the role of father of the bride at their wedding. He walked her up the aisle before making the most wonderful speech at their wedding reception in The Landmark Hotel in Carrick-on-Shannon in Co. Leitrim. He told stories about their dad and the happy times they had all shared over the years. Everyone in the room laughed and cried. It was the perfect tribute to Martin Cox senior who was so sorely missed. Seán wanted Sinéad to feel like their dad was part of her big day and she did. The Cox family were always very close, but I think the terribly premature death of Martin senior brought them even closer together.

Salty Chips and Christmas Trees

I'm always amazed by the random triggers that take you right back to your childhood. A song, a smell, a taste can send you travelling right back to a particular moment in time. I grew up in Walkinstown in Dublin and lived there until I was in my mid-twenties. My childhood was probably very typical of its time in seventies Ireland. I was born in 1965 and christened Martina Bannon. My mam, Ann, was a stay-at-home mam to me and my two sisters, Bernie and Catherine, and my two brothers, Patrick and Terence. My dad, Patrick, Patsy or Paddy (he answered to all three), was the local milkman. As a result, everyone knew the Bannons. My dad was a very hard worker: he was up at the crack of dawn and worked long days. He was someone who got an awful lot from his job; he enjoyed the link it gave him with everyone in our local community. From the time the five of us were very young he tried to instil that work ethic in us. He got us all involved in the milk run, even when none of us wanted to do it. Both my mam and dad were originally from Kells in Co. Meath and had moved to Walkinstown. My grandparents were still living in Kells, so every Sunday we'd go to visit them. Mam and Dad would pile the five of us into the back of the car and off we'd go. At Christmas time we'd spend the journey counting the Christmas trees in the windows of the houses, on either side of the road, totting up the number when we'd reach our destination.

We weren't deprived of anything when we were young, but it was a time when there wasn't a lot of money around. We were happy and didn't want for anything. I do remember one Christmas I got a school bag as a present. I laugh when I think about that and I wonder what one of my three children would think if Santa left a school bag, of all things. We never went on holiday abroad in those days; not many people did. We spent our summers in a rented house in Clare. Neither of my parents ever drank but they enjoyed going out to the movies together. They'd often bring us back a bag of chips from the chipper which felt like the biggest treat ever. We devoured those salty chips and I can still taste them now. Irish dancing was my passion and I spent most of childhood going to lessons and taking part in competitions. I adored it. My first dancing lessons were held in the front living room of our dance teacher's house. She later built a garage in her back garden, so we progressed there. My sisters took lessons originally too, but they eventually gave it up. I kept going and was still dancing at the age of 18. It was a great social outlet for us at a time when there wasn't a whole lot to do. My mam got to know the other 'dance mams' and it offered us a circle of friends in our community with a shared interest. It also afforded me an opportunity to travel for competitions, which I did many times over the years. It was always a great thrill to come away with a medal or a trophy.

Myself and my two sisters went to St Paul's School in Walkinstown, which was just 10 minutes from our house. The nuns at St Paul's ran a tight ship, ensuring everyone always walked on the right-hand side of the corridor. I was average at school – I didn't love it or hate it, I just turned up and did what I was asked to do. When I left secondary school, I had no idea what I wanted to do with my life. A third-level education wasn't high on the list of many people's priorities in 1980s Ireland; the focus was very much on getting a job. Many had witnessed huge poverty over that time, they'd seen their parents struggle to get by and most people just wanted to earn a decent living. The first Dublin branch of Dunnes Stores opened in 1957 on Henry Street in the city centre. As the years went on stores opened all over Ireland offering customers 'better value' food, fashion and homeware all under one roof. I decided I'd apply for a part-time job as a sales assistant in Kilnamanagh, until I decided what I really wanted to do. Little did I think back then that I'd spend more than three decades with the company. I can still see the big duffle coat I wore to the job interview. To this day I'm not sure how I got the job, but I did. In those early years different positions came up, they weren't advertised in the way they would be now, but word would get around, names would be put forward and people moved around the company. It didn't take me long to realise that I wanted to be a buyer and head office was where I needed to be. I had caught the bug so when a position came up, I decided to go for it, sure I had nothing to lose. I was quite shy but surprised myself and got the job. By the time I was 20, I was based in head office, which at the time was in an old building on George's

Street. I started in an administration role before moving on to be an assistant buyer in children's wear. Back then all staff members wore a uniform with a different colour and style signifying your progression through the company. I went from a gingham dress to a grey skirt with a maroon cardigan to finally a navy suit. The people who could wear their own clothes to work were the ones who had reached the top. It was a different time. Everything was done manually, and staff were addressed by their title and their surname.

My direct boss in those days was Ms Therese Dunne, the sister of my current boss, Mrs Margaret Heffernan. Therese was an amazing lady. She was one of the company directors and buyers and I learned so much from her over the years. One night I was working late, when she came into the room with a bouquet of flowers. 'You're engaged?' she asked. 'I am!' I replied. She handed me the flowers. 'Bring them home with you now and cause a bit of hassle – make sure he knows you've lots of admirers,' she said. She was a gas woman and a force to be reckoned with. I have nothing but fond memories of my time working with her. She passed away in 1995, long before her time. Working in Dunnes Stores has influenced my life in a lot of different ways. I grew up with the company and learned so much from the different people I came in contact with. I took it all in, watching closely how the most experienced operated. One of them was Dan Barrett, who was known as the first ever employee of Dunnes Stores. He was from Cork and had helped Ben Dunne Snr establish the company's first store on Patrick's Street in the city in 1944. He stayed with the company for 70 years. In those early days he oversaw the buying of socks. Twice a week he travelled from Cork to Dublin and it was my job to work with him. He was a very shrewd businessman who taught me a lot about buying. Back then most of the sock manufacturers were based in the UK so every so often we would have to travel over to visit all the suppliers and do a tour of the factories. When it came to negotiating a price, Mr Barrett often threw in a few words of Gaeilge to confuse everyone. It always worked too! He went on to be involved with the company right up until his death in 2014 at the age of 93.

Over the years I progressed up the ranks to become a buyer and there isn't a department in Dunnes Stores I haven't worked in. From children's wear to school uniforms, ladies' accessories to homewares, I've been involved in all of them. I learned on my feet and progressed from being a shy sales assistant to a buyer travelling around the world negotiating with suppliers. And I know how lucky I am to have always felt both fulfilled and challenged by my job. The company is now run by Mrs Margaret Heffernan and her family. Their aim remains a simple one: to deliver the best to their customers. Management hold their staff to very high standards. If you aren't performing, you'll be told. I remember one particular exchange with Mrs Heffernan years ago. I was making decisions on a range of ladies' accessories for the upcoming season. As a buyer you study the trends in the marketplace and then pick the handbags, hats and scarves that will eventually make it to the shop floor. It was a tricky department – a handbag is such a personal thing: you either like it or you don't. Nonetheless I picked the range meticulously as I always had but when I presented it to Mrs Heffernan, she wasn't overly enamoured. She had, and still has, a specific vision for the company which involves always offering something new and different; as she says herself, 'that is what the customer wants'. I loved the range, but to her it wasn't the best it could be. I came away from that range review reminding myself to go that extra mile next time.

Scarlet Fever

Seán and I were married for eight years before our first child, Jack came along. We hadn't planned it that way, it was just the way it worked out. Looking back now I feel lucky that we got to enjoy that time, just the two of us. Married life was lovely. We were both working hard but we enjoyed ourselves too. We socialised with different groups of friends and enjoyed weekends away and holidays. It was a carefree existence. We began a tradition of playing cards with my parents, Ann and Paddy, which we continued for years. We did it religiously every Thursday evening. Seán loved playing cards, as did my dad. I wasn't too pushed but I'd play along for a while then head off to the sitting room to watch television. They'd play away for hours and I always rejoined them for the last game of the night. And somehow, I'd always win. They'd all laugh at how I managed it. We never played for much money, but I'd always come away with the pot. Seán would say I was just lucky like that. One Christmas we decided to go all out with our gifts for one another. I can't remember what prompted the extravagance, but we planned to go big. I thought long and hard about what I might get

Seán before eventually deciding on a new golf bag. I couldn't wait to see his face when he got it. When Christmas morning rolled around, Seán woke me early. 'Happy Christmas,' he said as he handed me a tiny little package. I had no idea what could be inside. As I tore the paper off, I could see something silver. 'This can't be jewellery,' I said to myself. Seán was the first to admit he didn't have a great eye for jewellery, something we laughed about over the years. As I tore the final piece of paper off, I realised I was holding what looked like a car key. 'No, you didn't?' I said. He grabbed my hand and directed me to the bedroom window. 'Look' he said, pointing outside. Sitting on the road right in front of our house was a beautiful burgundy Opel Corsa. I couldn't believe my eyes. He had arranged for someone to park it there the night before when we were asleep. He had thought of everything. 'We said big, but I didn't mean a car!' I said as I ran down the stairs to go out and have a proper look. I felt awful handing over his golf bag, but he was delighted. The fact that he had pulled off such a surprise was enough for Seán. That was his way. He was so thoughtful and really enjoyed doing things for the people he loved. He never really wanted much for himself.

As much as we enjoyed those early years of married life, when our time was very much our own, we were absolutely thrilled when we discovered I was pregnant. We were more than ready for a baby. I had had a miscarriage just before so I was really nervous at first and spent a lot of time wondering would something go wrong again. But as the weeks passed by, I relaxed into it and let myself enjoy the pregnancy more and more. We started to talk about whether the baby would be a boy or a girl, we got excited about who he or she might look like, and we mulled over what names we liked. When Jack arrived in April 1997 everyone thought we named him after Seán, but we didn't. The local doctor who I went to for check-ups during my pregnancy always referred to the baby as 'little Jack'. We had no idea if we were having a boy or a girl, but at every appointment he'd ask 'Well, how's little Jack doing?' I had actually picked the name Robert if the baby was a boy. But the minute he was born, me and Seán just looked at each other and said, 'little Jack'. It had stuck. Our first daughter, Shauna, came along 17 months later so we had two under two. Shauna also wasn't named after Seán. I actually picked the name because I went to school with a girl whose sister's name was Shauna and I always thought it was a lovely name. Seán was so over the moon that we now had a little girl that I could have suggested any name under the sun.

At this stage Seán was working as a sales director with MK Electric and was mostly working from home in our attic which we had converted into an office. With two small children life was hectic. My work involved at least two big trips abroad a year. When Jack and Shauna were very young, I had to go on a buying trip to China, Singapore and India. The children were in a crèche and Seán was taking care of everything outside of the time they spent there. I'd ring every night to make sure everything was okay. 'All great,' he'd tell me night after night. It was only when I arrived back, I discovered both Jack and Shauna had contracted scarlet fever and had been out of crèche and at home with Seán the whole time. My sisters, Catherine and Bernie, had been dropping dinners to the door as Seán was also trying to work while minding two sick toddlers. But he managed. I wasn't a bit surprised he didn't tell me. 'Why worry about something if there is nothing you can do about it?' said Seán. And he was right.

Our third child, Emma, came along two and a half years after Shauna. Seán was and is a brilliant dad. He used to joke that I got all the praise for juggling being a mam and working full time and travelling. 'Where's my praise?' he'd say. 'I'm doing all the work.' But the truth of it was he really enjoyed his time with the children. He always got stuck in and was never afraid to take on his fair share of responsibilities. Seán's approach to everything in life has always been, 'If you're going to do something give it your commitment one hundred per cent'. And his approach to being a dad was no different from that. He has had the most wonderful relationship with all three of them from the time they were born. Children love someone with a sense of humour and Seán has that in spades. He was a messer and they grew up laughing along with him. When they started going to school, if one of them wouldn't get out of bed on time he'd go into the room and tickle them until they got up. He had special names for the girls: Shauna was 'Milly the Minx' and Emma 'Gilly the Goose'. I've no idea how or why he came up with those names, but they often communicated in this secret language. 'John Barnes' was another name he used to throw around in conversation with the girls. He'd say it randomly in the middle of a sentence, like 'Hurry up or I'll get John Barnes'. Emma thought John Barnes was a figment of her dad's imagination, that he had just made him up. I remember her face when she saw the real John Barnes, the famous former Liverpool player, on a poster at Anfield. 'He's an actual person!' she exclaimed in disbelief. Seán's relationship with the kids was and still is very unique and very special. He was strict with them too, particularly about their education. As they got a bit older he became really hands-on with their schoolwork. He recognised the importance of them doing well and took a great interest in their different subjects. If one of them found a particular subject difficult, he'd patiently sit at the table with them for hours trying to help them figure it out. He pushed them to do well and I think all three of them were motivated to succeed because of his encouragement. He wasn't hard on them and he didn't have unrealistic expectations; all he wanted was for them to achieve their personal best. When Shauna was in Sixth Year of secondary school and studying for her Leaving Cert, he'd say, 'Show me that study timetable so I can see you're doing enough.' When Emma was doing her Junior Cert and came down to the kitchen for a snack he'd ask, 'What are you doing down here again?' He was joking really but he wanted them to know he was keeping a close eye on them.

Seán also really encouraged the children when it came to their hobbies. From the minute Jack showed an interest in GAA, Seán supported him. He was his number one fan, but he didn't go easy on him. Seán didn't dance around his feedback and as Jack got older, if he had a bad game after a night out, he got no free passes from Seán. When on the pitch, Jack could always hear one voice in the crowd over everyone else's and that was his dad shouting from the sidelines. I don't think Seán ever missed one of Jack's matches. The pair of them never missed a Dublin match either – from the time Jack could walk Seán brought him along to cheer on the Dubs. A massive love of Liverpool was also passed down from father to son, and both of them absolutely loved going to watch the Reds play. Seán had this little backpack that he brought to all the matches. It was the ugliest thing but he didn't care; it carried everything he needed. They'd put their sandwiches and bags of crisps in, and off they'd go. Over the years they were lucky enough to enjoy many trips to Anfield. Seán brought Jack to matches from the time he was old enough to go. Sometimes they'd travel over on the morning of a match and come home that evening, tired but happy. On other occasions they went off for the night, taking a flight the evening before a match. They'd go for something to eat and then watch a movie in their hotel room. Jack has years of very happy memories with his dad at Anfield.

Seán was really opinionated and our kitchen table became a great place for a heated debate. Himself and Shauna could argue for hours over a contentious topic. He knew how to push her buttons, but she was well able for him. They'd eventually run out of steam and go their separate ways. Seán would later come back with his tail between his legs to make peace. He was a dad who always loved spending time with the children. He was also clued in with what was going on in their lives. In fact, it was Seán who first guessed Jack had a girlfriend. One night he arrived home from our local pub, where Jack and Laura worked, with the news. 'I'm telling you,' he said, 'there's definite chemistry between those two.' His suspicions were confirmed sometime later when Jack introduced us to his girlfriend Laura. Seán had an instinct about things like that, just like he knew deep down it was better not to tell me about the scarlet fever when I was so far away.

Our Forever Home

'Is that it now, are you sure you've finally settled?' asked my mam hopefully when myself and Seán decided in 2000 to make the move from Dublin to Dunboyne in Co. Meath. It was going to be our fourth time to move since we had gotten married in 1989. For some reason unknown to me, I had never settled in our first home, the bungalow we had bought from my sister in Clondalkin. We sold it and moved to a three-bedroomed semi-detached house, also in Clondalkin, where we stayed for a few years, before moving to Ballycullen where we lived when both Jack and Shauna were born. 'Yes, Mam, this is definitely our final move,' I assured her. I knew this was going to be our 'forever home'. With two small children and a lot of toys we had outgrown the house in Ballycullen. We needed more space. House prices were high at the time, but we started to look around at what was on offer. Seán was working with Kellihers Electrical which was based in Ballymount but he was on the road quite regularly, so he began to investigate the possibility of moving outside of Dublin but close enough to the city to commute to work. One day he mentioned to me that he had come across a property in Dunboyne that he really liked. I had been thinking more along the lines of Lucan. 'Meath?' I said. 'Sure I'm not moving to Meath, we work in Dublin.' It seemed as far away from Dublin as Cork at that point. But Seán being Seán convinced me to go and have a look.

Cleverly he brought me to see the house on a Sunday when there was no traffic on the roads. Seán was pushy and if he truly believed in something he'd always try hard to get me on board. His trick worked! 'That took no time at all,' I remarked as we pulled up to an unfinished housing estate. The house Seán had his eye on was Number 3 on a row of four houses at the front of the estate, which had around 60 houses in total. It had everything we were looking for: a spacious back garden for the children, a garage and four bedrooms. Like all projects Seán took on, he had done his research. He knew everything there was to know about the local schools, the shops, the sporting facilities and of course the local pubs! We had no link whatsoever to Dunboyne and we didn't know one person living in the village or surrounding areas but there was no argument. It really did tick all the boxes. The decision was made. We were moving away from Dublin to Dunboyne in Co. Meath. Looking back on that time now, I can safely say it was the best decision we ever made. Dunboyne is unique in the sense that it's quite a big place, but it has a real village feel to it. It took us no time to settle in. The housing estate was new, so a residents' association was formed. Seán of course became the first chairman of the new group. He got everyone together to organise grass cutting and other bits of upkeep that needed to be done. We got to know our neighbours, Edel and John, who are now our close friends. But, as is the case with so many communities around Ireland, it was when we became involved with our local GAA club, St Peter's, that we truly put down roots in Dunboyne. Seán couldn't wait to get down there and as soon as Jack could run Seán took him by the hand to investigate what was on offer. And it just went from there. Before long Seán and Jack were completely sucked in. Those Sunday morning kickarounds when Jack was very small turned into junior leagues, matches and away games. Families came together to transport children back and forth to games, to make tea and coffee, to wash jerseys and to offer support. We were meeting the same people week in, week out with the same goal.

I still remember the night, years later, when Seán arrived home with the news that a new chairman was being elected at St Peter's. 'My name has been put forward,' he said, sounding shocked. I wasn't a bit surprised. Seán was obsessed with the GAA and the comings and goings at the club. He took on the role of chairman in 2013 and threw himself fully into it. It was a time of great change for the club: St Peter's was growing rapidly. Seán played an important role in guiding the club through that transformation. His mission was to bring as many people into the club as possible, because he truly saw it as the heartbeat of the community. He was really dedicated to the role, always committing one hundred per cent to the challenge. Seán set time aside to get all his paperwork in order before each meeting. There is still a big file in our house bursting with GAA notes from over the years. The role of chairman can be a difficult one; there's always some issue that needs to be addressed, and there are always lots of differing points of view to be considered. Seán has always been stubborn, and I think that personality trait really helped him to get things done. There was also a lot of peacemaking involved over the years but Seán is a very calm person, so that helped him to keep a cool head during the tricky times. He worked hard in that role but he got as much back as he put in. When we first moved to Dunboyne our link with St Peter's GAA Club gave us a huge sense of solidarity and belonging. When Seán and Jack first became immersed in the GAA club I introduced Shauna and Emma to Irish dancing. Seán would say to me, 'You won't be happy until the girls are dancing like you did,' but I never forced them into it. They both loved it and are still dancing. Seán didn't have a huge interest in it but he never let that stop him from encouraging and supporting the two girls. 'Do it for you,' he'd say to them for encouragement as they headed off to whatever competition they were taking part in. Seán wanted everyone to do their best, to reach their potential. I've no doubt that as Seán stood on all those sidelines over the years with Jack, his own tradition with his dad supporting Roscommon years beforehand was at the front of his mind. And as I sat for hours on end in different dance halls around the country watching Shauna and Emma dance, I too was remembering my own childhood. We were both making new memories based very much on old ones.

Happy Friday

At five o'clock on a Friday evening Seán usually went to our local pub, Slevin's in Dunboyne. Nothing, and I mean nothing, would get in the way of this tradition – in fact, it was like part of Seán's religion. Life was hectic; we were both working full time and rearing three children. Ozzie had also joined our household, our first Jack Russell. As soon as Jack, Shauna and Emma could talk, they started asking us could we get a dog. 'No, maybe next year,' we'd say to the chorus of pleas. I thought they were too young and we were busy enough as it was. 'What happens when the novelty wears off?' I'd ask them. I knew the answer. I would be left to look after the dog. But they kept it up and lobbied hard over the years. By the time they reached the ages of 9, 11 and 12 I started to change my mind. Maybe now they were old enough. I brought it up with Seán and he agreed. We'd get a dog. That Christmas we got a piece of paper and wrote down different letters on it. We cut them up and put them into an envelope. When they woke on Christmas morning we told them we had a riddle that they had to unscramble. They had no idea what was going on. They carefully opened the envelope and poured the letters onto the table. One by one they moved them around, putting them in different orders to see what it spelt. Then they got it. M-A-D-R-A. 'Madra!' they shouted in unison. 'We're getting a madra!' The excitement. They were over the moon. We waited until the hustle and bustle of Christmas had passed before Ozzie came to live with us. I shouldn't have worried. He was the most adored dog in the country, walked twice a day and smuggled into one of the kids beds' at nighttime.

Over the years we had the most wonderful childminder, Síle Hutchinson, who helped us in so many ways, but the weeks went by in a haze of work and school, lunches, homework, activities and Ozzie. Someone always needed to be somewhere. When you're in that busy bubble that so many parents who work outside the home experience, you can never imagine not having so much to do. Our weekends were still filled with GAA matches and Irish dancing and whatever the kids had on the go, but as they got older it became a lot less hectic. My work was still taking me away on two big buying trips a year, mostly at this stage to India. Seán was working as a sales director with Precision Cables in Dundalk but also spent a lot of time travelling to different parts of the country. Every Friday he had the exact same routine – he was a real creature of habit. He'd finish up work early, around 3 p.m. First things first, he'd hop up on the bed for a little rest after a hectic week. At around 5 p.m. he'd get up and saunter down to Slevin's in the village. There he'd meet up with the locals to right the world over a few pints. The same familiar faces – week in, week out. He loved the familiarity of it all. He knew everyone, and everyone knew

Seán. I have always been quite reserved, but Seán was sociable. He was shy, too, though and reserved in some situations. But he really enjoyed chatting to people and had a great ability to find common ground with whoever he met. When we were out together I'd say to him, 'What were you talking to that fella about?' and I always got the same answer: 'Sport'. I guess when you have a passion for sport, which Seán had in spades, you're never short of a conversation starter. Seán lived for those Friday nights in Slevin's. By half-past eight he'd toddle back home so we could eat together. Friday night was takeaway night in our house, and it still is. Jack, Shauna and Emma were beginning to live their own lives so they wouldn't always be there. Seán loved a good Indian or a nice pizza from our local Italian restaurant, La Bucca in Dunboyne. He'd always order the 'Don Aldo' pizza which has shredded duck on it, and he adored it. We'd order the food and pour a glass of wine. Seán never really wanted the wine after having a few pints, but he'd always agree to have a glass with me to be sociable. By ten o'clock most Friday nights he'd be falling asleep in front of *The Late Late Show* with most of the wine spilled down his shirt. They were just normal run-of-the-mill Friday nights, together after a busy week. We wanted for nothing; just to be together. It's strange now when I look back at something so ordinary, something we took for granted, something we thought would happen every Friday night, until it didn't.

Seán also developed a love for golf, and he started to play most Saturday mornings at Carton House Golf Course in Maynooth with a group of friends. He really enjoyed it. For his 50th birthday he organised a golfing trip to Portugal with his brothers and friends. His birthday is 9 April, so it coincided with the Masters Tournament. They got T-shirts printed with the Masters logo and someone got their hands on a green blazer for the winner. They played golf all day, then went for dinner, then watched the real Masters that night. It was a dream trip for all of them and was such a success they did it again for Seán's 51st, 52nd and 53rd birthdays. I know if things were different he would have continued that tradition for years to come. Most Saturday nights we'd meet our friends Richard and Una or James and Deborah for dinner or have people over to the house. Seán considered himself the king of the barbeque and he loved entertaining at home. Cooking a nice steak, a cold can of beer in hand, with family and friends around was all he ever really wanted. Even when we did go out for dinner Seán would always prefer to stay local. We'd slag him over not wanting to go too far. There was a method to his madness, though – it meant no matter where we went, we'd be back to Slevin's in time for a proper pint of Guinness.

Hurricane Sandy and Our Secret

In 2014 myself and Seán celebrated our 25th wedding anniversary. Because it was a big one, we decided to push the boat out – literally. I had always wanted to go on a cruise, but Seán wasn't too gone on the idea. When he was a child a group of lads threw him in a river. He wasn't injured and he managed to get himself out of the water, but he was left with a lifelong fear of water. As a result he never learned to swim. When the children were young he went for swimming lessons, determined to battle his demons. He really wanted to be able to swim with the kids when we were on holiday. He did well but he never really got comfortable in the water and would mostly just float around on his back. Nonetheless I really wanted to do something big to mark the fact that we had been married for a quarter of a century, a milestone celebration. It struck me that we had been married now longer than I had been alive when I first met him. I thought a cruise would be the perfect treat, and I was confident he would enjoy it once we were there. So, I did what Seán would do, got some brochures and left them around the house, and sure enough he came around to the idea. We'd only ever been away for a weekend without the kids, so it was a big deal to leave them for eight nights, but they were teenagers at this stage with lots of people to keep an eye on them. It was a Mediterranean cruise which started in Barcelona and I remember vividly Seán holding my hand tightly when we were boarding the ship. It was so unlike him; he couldn't look down at the water. I was thinking maybe this wasn't a great idea but once he was on board, he relaxed.

The cruise stopped off in Spain, France and Italy, taking in all the breathtaking sights as we went along. Messina in Italy was our favourite stop-off, it was stunning. On the last day we paid extra to spend the day on the posh upper deck of the ship. We knew we'd be back home soon enough, so we said we'd splash out. It was worth it. We were treated like royalty for the day, sitting by the pool being waited on hand and foot. We reminisced a lot about how wonderful our wedding day had been. We also remembered the hard times in the months straight after and how lucky we had been to have Seán's dad, Martin senior, and his Uncle Ken there on the day to celebrate with us. The fact that we had lost both of them so soon after the wedding, as well as Seán's cousin Stephen, still shocked us, all these years later. You really never know what life has in store for you. We also talked about how young we had both been. At this stage Jack was nearly 20 years old, the age I was when I first met Seán. 'Imagine if Jack arrived home to tell us he was getting married,' said Seán and we both laughed at the idea. We really had been babies. By the time we got to our 30th wedding anniversary things would be very different. I will always be grateful that we had that time together on the cruise, that we pressed pause on our busy lives and made sure we celebrated the milestone.

In fact, I take solace in all the wonderful happy holiday memories I hold dearly from over the years. Before we ever had children, Lapland was on our bucket list. I'd say to Seán, 'If we have kids, and we can afford it, we have to take them to see the real Santa,' and when the time was right, we did it. Dressed from head to toe in our snow suits, the five of us spent the days trekking around the snowy forest. After a bite to eat and a drink we'd head back to our cosy log cabin where we'd light the fire and settle in for the night. The kids were all at the perfect age. I'll never forget the looks on their faces when they met the real Santa. It was truly the most magical experience and I'll never forget it. We also used to take the kids camping in France when they were very young. We'd hire a car and head off for a fortnight. Seán was always the driver, he liked to be in control of that. 'Driving Miss Daisy' was what he'd call me to which I'd remind him he was happy enough for me to drive when he wanted to have a few drinks. The slagging and joking has always been warm and good natured. We just got on so well.

Even the trips that didn't go according to plan are now treasured memories that I'll be forever grateful for. In 2012 we took what was to be the trip of a lifetime to New York. Unbelievably, we landed in the city that never sleeps at the same time as Hurricane Sandy. The five of us were staying on the 27th floor of a hotel on 34th Street. We ended up in lockdown for five days, unable to go anywhere. We were watching the coverage of the storm on our television in our room while hotel staff were putting letters under the door telling us not to go outside. We ate breakfast, lunch and dinner in a little diner attached to the hotel. But we made the most of it. As we were told to batten down the hatches, we curled up into the two double beds in the room and passed the time playing cards, using Skittles for money, and chatting for hours. The children were at that stage where they wanted to know what life was like when we were younger. I think there's a natural curiosity in children to know what on earth their parents did before they became the parents. So, we answered their questions and spent the time reminiscing about life in what they called the 'olden days'. We told them how their Auntie Suzanne had introduced us and how Seán had come along to my 21st birthday party. They got a great laugh out of the fact that I hated their dad's sleeveless pullover jumpers and that Seán had to walk from Clondalkin to Walkinstown to see me. They also couldn't believe how quickly we had gotten engaged and then married and how young we had been. The stories kept us occupied – sure what else could we do? We were in constant contact with Aer Lingus checking for flights, but as the storm raged on there were no planes landing or taking off. After a few days the worst of Sandy passed, and we could venture out to a little pizzeria beside the hotel. It was a welcome relief from the diner. It was there as we tucked into a jumbo pizza that the conversation continued. Jack said, 'Tell us something you've never told us, something we don't know – tell us a secret.' I remember the moment like it was yesterday. Seán and I just looked at one another. We didn't say anything but we both knew this was the right time. What the children didn't know was that when I was pregnant with Emma seven years earlier, we had been told we were expecting twins. We were shocked, but delighted. However, our joy was short-lived. Before long the doctors realised I was having what's called a molar pregnancy, a condition where a non-viable egg implants but doesn't come to term. It was a worrying time as I had also been told the other baby, Emma, may not survive. Thankfully she was perfectly healthy, weighing in at 10 pounds, but sadly the other baby was not to be. Over the years Seán and I had talked about when we might tell the children, but we just didn't know when the right time might be. It turned out it was over pizza in New York as Storm Sandy moved into the distance. I can still see their faces; they were completely gobsmacked and left wondering what other secrets we had. We assured them that was the height of it. After the initial shock there was lots of joking and slagging over what life would have been like with two Emmas.

As the kids got older we started to go to Liverpool more often as a family. Seán and Jack had gone numerous times over the years; the two of them were well bonded in their shared love for the club. But they had mostly just gone on quick trips, to watch a match and come home again. In December 2017, we planned a trip to Liverpool for the five of us as a family. We got the Saturday morning red-eye flight and landed in the city before it had even woken up. Seán took us for breakfast and we checked in to an apartment we had booked for a few days. It was located right in the middle of the city and within walking distance of everywhere we wanted to go. Seán and Jack headed off for Anfield while me and the girls went for lunch and did a bit of shopping. Later on we all met up for dinner. It was the first time we'd been in Liverpool when all three of them were teenagers and old enough to enjoy a meal out. We had such a wonderful time just being in each other's company in the city that was such a big part of our lives, not realising that in a few short months our lives would change forever.

Falling in Love With Lagos

I n 2004 we discovered our home away from home, Portugal. It was a paradise of sunshine, relaxing by the pool, beautiful beaches and most importantly quality time together as a family after another busy year. Coming up to the summer of 2004, we'd been looking for somewhere new to go for our annual summer holiday. A few people had recommended Portugal, but I didn't really know too much about it. Seán was a great organiser and he loved taking on a project. He was the same in his circle of friends. He'd often suggest a golfing trip with a group of pals and once they agreed he'd be the one to organise everything. He'd check the flights and find somewhere for them to stay before reporting back the details. He enjoyed seeing a plan come together and I know his friends really enjoyed those trips over the years. So, off he went to the local travel agent in Dunboyne village where he quizzed the woman working there on what Portugal had to offer. She recommended the Villa Branca Apartments in Lagos to him. It was a family-friendly complex a short walk from the beach and the centre of the town. She didn't over-sell it and told Seán it was quite basic but was a massive hit with families. So, we decided to take a chance and book a two-week stay that July. Little did we know then that Portugal would become such a massive part of our lives. It was like the greatest love affair – we were completely smitten.

As soon as the holiday was over, we booked to go back the following year, and the following year again, and then every July for the next 13 years. We loved it and so did the children. We'd usually book an early morning flight out of Dublin, meaning all going according to plan we'd be settled in the apartment by midday. We'd hire a car which would almost buckle under the weight of the five of us and our luggage. As we made our way to Lagos we'd chat about the holiday to come, the people we'd meet up with, the restaurants we'd eat in. Seán would tease the girls over packing a different bikini for every day and they'd blame the lack of space on his golf clubs which had to lie across their legs until we reached our destination. The holiday started immediately. I'd unpack and Seán and the kids would go to the local supermarket to stock up for the fortnight. The sun was shining and the days by the pool or the beach were chilled and easy. At night we'd take our pick of the many incredible restaurants, which we became so familiar with over the years. I'd sometimes suggest eating in, but Seán wouldn't hear of it. 'Sure, we can do that at home,' he'd say. 'Come on – we're on holiday.' Life was for living, according to Seán. Over the years different family members and close friends would join us in Lagos, and we made some lifelong friends there too, as did the children. Seán and I felt very comfortable and safe there, so we gave them a lot of freedom which they really enjoyed. Before long it just became part of our annual routine. We went to Villa Branca in July and that was it. As soon as we arrived home from one trip, we began to look forward to the next one. No matter how busy or hectic the year was, all five of us looked forward to our holiday in Portugal.

One day when Jack was in Sixth Class of primary school he arrived home with big news. He was part of a team chosen to play at Croke Park at half time of a Dublin Vs Louth match. He announced the date in July and I just looked at Seán – it was right in the middle of our Portugal holiday. 'How will we manage that?' I asked, immediately stressing about the logistics. But nothing was a problem for Seán. 'It's simple,' he said. 'We're not missing either.' And they didn't. We all flew out to Portugal and then a week later Seán and Jack flew home on the Saturday night so Jack could play the match on the Sunday. By Sunday night they were back in Portugal. At this stage news had reached us that Jack's team had won. Jack had scored and when they arrived back at the bar we were having a drink in, Jack still in his GAA gear, he was welcomed with a massive cheer. Years later, at 18 years of age and having just completed his Leaving Certificate, Jack joined us in Portugal after his coming-of-age holiday with his friends. He was a little dishevelled, but nothing was going to get in the way of his Portugal holiday. Shauna did the same the year she finished secondary school. Even as young adults the children didn't want to miss it. It was just our happy place. It's hard to put into words how much we enjoyed our time there over the years. One night walking home from dinner we found ourselves looking in the window of a property agent's and the dream began of maybe one day owning our own home in Lagos. We started to talk about it more and more. I'm not sure I would have been the one to try to make that dream a reality. Seán was always the proactive one in terms of those really big life decisions. When we arrived back from our last holiday there in July 2017 Seán said to me, 'We keep talking about this, let's just do something about it.'

Before long he had contacted a few property agents and the flights were booked for the following February. We had a wish list; we knew we wanted somewhere within walking distance of the town and near to the beach, we didn't want anything high rise and we hoped for two or three bedrooms as we really wanted this to be a base for friends and family too and for the children and their friends. We had arrived at that stage in life when you start to contemplate the next 20 years. A time when maybe we wouldn't have to work as hard as we had through the years. A time when our children would all become adults. The next phase of our lives together. An itinerary was set up which involved looking at around six properties over two days. We'd been given the details before we travelled so we had spent a bit of time researching each place online, but we couldn't wait to view them properly. Off we set, excited about the prospect of making this dream a reality. We went to view the properties and, just like when myself and Seán met, when you know you know. We were unanimous in our decision. This apartment had everything we'd been looking for and more. It was located on the opposite end of Lagos to Villa Branca but was around a 15-minute walk into the town, it was up a lovely hill with two big double balconies and a pool, and it was fully furnished. We couldn't believe our luck. It was perfect. We said we'd sleep on it, after all it was a massive decision, but that night we went out to celebrate. Our heads had already gone there, and there was talk of heading out for New Year's Eve, the Easter holidays and some of the bank holiday weekends. The following morning, we paid a deposit on our future home away from home. A few weeks later Seán was back in Portugal for what had become the annual 'Coxy's Masters' golf trip with his friends. He travelled to Lagos and opened a bank account and met with our solicitor who was dealing with the contracts for the sale. We then booked two flights for May, a trip that would see us close the sale making our dream a reality. But by the time May arrived Seán was in a coma in The Walton Centre in Liverpool. The dream had become a nightmare.

A Kiss Goodbye

Tuesday 24 April 2018 began like any other day, but by the time the sun had set our lives had changed forever. I was woken early by Seán coming around to my side of the bed to kiss me goodbye. He was heading to Dublin Airport to catch his red-eye flight to Liverpool. A few days beforehand his younger brother Marty had managed to get two tickets to the Champions League semi-final tie between Liverpool and Roma FC. Trips to watch his beloved Liverpool were a very regular occurrence for Seán. For as long as I had known him he went to Anfield twice or three times every year. But this was different: it was the game of the season. Four days beforehand Marty was walking through the reception of MJ Flood Limited, the office equipment supplier he worked for, when the managing director called him over to tell him he had two tickets for the match. 'I can't make it, they're yours if you want them,' he said. Marty couldn't believe it. Tickets for European nights at Anfield were like gold dust. Liverpool had been gaining momentum and were edging closer to a sixth European title. This was an incredible stroke of luck! Marty wasn't sure if he could make it work, though – his son Billy was due to make his Confirmation the day after the match. He rang his wife, Ruth, to fill her in on what had happened and to see what she thought about him travelling to the game. She agreed it was a once-in-a-lifetime opportunity and said she'd no issue at all once Marty was home early the following morning for the Confirmation mass, which was due to be held at midday. Once he'd gotten that far he went out to his car to call Seán. 'How did you manage that, ya jammy fecker?' asked Seán when Marty explained he'd gotten his hands on two tickets for the Roma game. He broke the good news. 'You're coming with me, Seán, we're both going.' Seán was over the moon. He took charge of getting the flights booked and Marty said he'd book accommodation. A few minutes later Marty got a text from Seán: 'Flights booked'. They couldn't believe their luck. Seán was carrying the little backpack he took to every match with him as he stood at my side of the bed and kissed me goodbye. 'Check in with you later,' he said as he headed out the door.

It was a busy time for me at work. I was in the middle of presenting Dunnes Stores' plans for Christmas 2018, always a hectic time of the year when you work in retail. The previous day I asked Seán to remind me to post paperwork to do with the new apartment in Portugal; I was afraid I'd forget about it with being so preoccupied with work. Later that morning Seán sent me a text to say himself and Marty had landed safely, they were having breakfast and he reminded me not to forget the post. I got a second text later in the day to say they were having lunch and then heading to the match. I got home from work that evening at around half-past six.

Normally I would go running on a Tuesday evening, but for some reason I decided to give it a miss. Rain was usually the only thing that would keep me indoors, but this particular April evening was dry and bright and mild, so I don't know why I made the decision to stay at home. Emma was gone Irish dancing, Shauna was upstairs studying, and Jack had just arrived home from training. He was sitting in the living room eating his dinner getting ready to watch the match on TV. The match his dad was at.

I was at the island in the kitchen when my mobile rang. It was Seán's sister-in-law, Aisling. It wasn't unusual for her to ring me, so I didn't think anything of it. 'Hi, Aisling,' I said into the phone. I knew immediately from the tone of her voice that something wasn't right. 'Martina,' she said, 'Seán has been in an accident.' An image of Seán kissing me goodbye as he left the house that morning popped into my head. He'd been in contact throughout the day – there must be a mistake. 'What do you mean?' I said. I suddenly felt like she was holding back, not telling me everything she knew. 'What accident?' I demanded. 'We don't have a lot of detail, but Seán was hit in the head, he's been taken to hospital,' she replied. To this day I have no idea exactly what I said to her, but I do remember saying, 'What … what, why are you ringing me?' The information just made no sense to me. She told me Peter, her husband and Seán's brother, was in the car on his way to my house and would be with me soon. Shauna heard my raised voice from upstairs and arrived down to see what was going on. Jack came in from the living room. 'Your dad's been injured,' I said to them. We were all shell-shocked. Shauna rang Emma. 'Don't ask Mam to collect you, okay? Just come on home,' she said to her. Emma was on her way. I started pacing around the kitchen island. I told myself to stay calm: 'Don't panic, Martina, there's been a mistake.' We weren't really saying anything; the three of us just kept walking up and down the kitchen. I remember Jack was really putting on a brave face. He kept saying he was sure that Seán had just gotten a dig or a nudge and maybe he needed an ice pack or at worst a few stitches.

Before long Peter arrived at the house. Detail was still thin on the ground. Seán and Marty hadn't turned up to The Twelfth Man pub to meet the man who was giving them their tickets. The man had contacted Marty's boss, who had in turn contacted Ruth. Immediately Ruth knew something wasn't right. She couldn't think of any good reason why Seán and Marty would not pick up their tickets. She finally got through to Marty on his phone. At this stage he was in the back of an ambulance with Seán on their way to Aintree University Hospital. I then remember Emma coming home from Irish dancing. I burst into tears as I met her at the front door. The house started to fill up with people. More family members, some of our neighbours and friends arrived. No one really knew what to say, people made tea, it was all a bit of a blur. I was brought back to reality when my mobile rang again. I recognised the 0044 number to be a UK one. 'Is this Martina Cox?' said the voice on the other end. 'Yes,' I said. She went on to tell me she was the nurse who had tended to Seán at Aintree University Hospital. She calmly told me that Seán had been brought to the hospital's emergency department after being assaulted outside Anfield stadium. She said he had been assessed and the decision had been made to transfer him to The Walton Centre, which was close by. I heard her say something about neurological experts and then she said, 'Seán will be taken for emergency surgery – he has a bleed on the brain'. At that point the room spun, and I thought I was going to be sick. 'Is he dead?' I screamed into the phone. The nurse told me he wasn't but that the next 24 hours would be crucial, and I should make my way to Liverpool as soon as possible. All my efforts to stay calm evaporated, as did the hope it had all been a mistake, that somehow, we had been misinformed. I was sure this couldn't be as bad as it seemed and now it looked like it was worse than I had even let myself imagine. Seán kissing me goodbye at the side of the bed seemed like only an hour ago. Yet now he was fighting for his life in hospital. How could this have happened? Going to Anfield was something he had done hundreds of times; it was a safe and familiar place for Seán.

The mood in the house changed after that phone call. Jack, Shauna and Emma had been standing around me when I'd spoken to the nurse. Everyone now knew how bad it was and everyone started to panic. I surrendered to those around me; there was nothing else I could do. Plans were made. It was decided that Peter would come to Liverpool with me but at this stage it was around 9 p.m. Aisling booked the next available flight for us, which was the first flight the next morning. Shauna and Emma set about packing me a bag. What do you put into a bag for your mam who is getting on a plane to be with your dad who may not survive the night? How long would I be gone for? What did I need? One of them packed a bottle of Rescue Remedy. I used to give them both a few drops of it to settle their nerves on the morning of a big dancing competition. I was going to need more than Rescue Remedy to get me through this though. Later that night the attack was reported on Sky Sports. Jack was watching. 'A man is in a critical condition after being attacked outside Anfield,' the reporter said. That night was the longest of my life. I spent the hours pacing up and down, counting the minutes until I could get to Seán, to see what had happened with my own eyes, to tell him everything would be okay. It felt like he was a million miles away. Everyone wanted me to get some rest, but I just couldn't close my eyes. This was a nightmare, and I was wide awake.

AFTER

The Walton Centre

I nside Anfield, Liverpool CEO Peter Moore had just taken his seat to watch the match. He looked around at the crowd. There were more than 50,000 people in the stadium and the atmosphere was electric. Liverpool was playing for its place in the Champions League Final. This was a big one, so everyone was nervous. As Peter settled into his seat and the game kicked off, he got a tap on the shoulder, a move that generally indicates bad news, or that his attention is needed elsewhere. It was the club's chief operations officer, Andy Hughes. 'We need you in the operations room,' said Andy. Peter didn't need to hear more; he stood up, excused himself and followed Andy. A short time earlier reports of an incident outside the stadium had started to circulate on social media. People were reporting that a Liverpool fan had been injured outside The Albert Pub. At first it was just a few tweets but then people started to share short video clips of what looked like a serious attack. Around 14 members of the club's Crisis Management Team convened in the operations room as efforts were made to verify the reports. Before long the Merseyside Police confirmed that a group of around

60 'ultra' or hardcore Roma fans had arrived onto Walton Breck Road, where the pub is located, from a side street. A Liverpool fan had been attacked and injured. He had been taken by ambulance to a nearby hospital.

Early in the morning after the attack, when Seáns brother Peter picked me up to go to Dublin Airport to get our flight to Liverpool, the first thing he said to me was, 'Don't look at your phone. It's everywhere.' News about Seán had spread quickly with reports circulating all over social media. As we travelled along the M50 with the radio on in the background, the news came on. 'A 53-year-old man from Dunboyne in Co. Meath has been seriously injured in an assault outside Anfield stadium in Liverpool,' announced the newsreader. It was such a surreal moment. Every few minutes my phone beeped, another message from someone hearing the news. 'Martina, I've just heard – tell me it's not Coxy.' Everyone was so shocked at what had happened; people couldn't believe it. I couldn't believe it. I wished I could tell them it wasn't true, that it wasn't Coxy, that it had all been a big mistake. I wished it wasn't true, but it was. We made our way through airport security and to our boarding gate in a complete daze. Neither Peter nor I had slept or eaten anything. We both ordered coffees on the plane, but we just sat there looking at them, unable to even drink anything.

By eight o'clock we had arrived at the hospital Seán had been taken to in Liverpool, The Walton Centre. A place I never imagined I'd need to visit – why would I? It's situated on the same site as Aintree University Hospital where Seán had been taken by ambulance after the attack. It's a specialist hospital dedicated to treating brain injuries. We made our way into the small building and were shown to a waiting room. The lights were off in the room so as I turned to walk in, I hit the light switch. It was then my eyes fell on Marty, Seán's brother. There he was, sitting in the corner of the room with his head in his hands. I will never forget that image. He looked broken. I rushed over to him and took him in my arms. He was completely devastated and shook. At this stage I had no idea of the real horror of what Seán and Marty had been through and it all felt too raw to even ask him. I knew that would all come later. Marty had travelled to Aintree University Hospital in the back of the ambulance with Seán. When the decision was made to transfer Seán the short distance to The Walton Centre, a nurse had walked Marty across a little land bridge to be with him. He had sat in the dark all night while Seán was in surgery. My heart broke for him in that moment. Two brothers had been doing something they loved to do together, supporting their beloved Liverpool – something they had done hundreds of times before. How did it go so wrong? As we sat with Marty, a member of the medical team came in to meet us and introduced us to Paul Eldridge, the hospital's professor of neurosurgery, who was looking after Seán. When he began to outline Seán's injuries, he didn't beat around the bush.

Seán had been assaulted outside Anfield stadium and had received a blow to the right side of his head. He had suffered an acute subdural haematoma and had needed surgery to relieve the pressure on his brain. Professor Eldridge explained that Seán had made it through the surgery and was now in the intensive care unit in an induced coma. 'Seán is very unwell. The next few hours will be critical,' he said. There was no sugar-coating Seán's condition. He explained that between 50 and 90 per cent of people who suffer an injury like this die from the condition or its complications. It was touch and go as to whether Seán would even make it through the next few hours and days. 'If he survives this it will change his life forever,' warned Professor Eldridge. As I watched the professor's mouth move I couldn't quite process what he was saying. Only a few hours before, Seán had been standing beside my bed, perfectly healthy. A voice in my head was shouting, 'You're wrong, maybe you're wrong,' but deep down I knew he wasn't. I was desperate to see Seán. To believe it I had to see it with my own eyes. But at the same time, I was terrified. Once I saw him, I knew I could no longer tell myself it wasn't true. A nurse arrived to prepare me to enter the ICU, and I was given a gown. I needed help putting it on, I was shaking so badly. We walked down to the ICU towards the double doors. I held my breath as we walked through them. I will never forget the scene inside. Nothing could have prepared me for it.

In the first bed on the right-hand side lay Seán. But he didn't look like Seán, not the Seán who had kissed me goodbye 24 hours earlier. This was a different Seán. A Seán who had returned badly injured from a war zone. His head was swollen and bandaged, and he was wearing a skull cap. He had wires and tubes coming out of him and a variety of different machines were beeping as they kept him alive. It was like a scene from a movie and it took my breath away. I stared at my once happy and healthy husband now helpless in this bed in intensive care. I kept looking at him, trying to take it all in. A nurse stood at the other side of the bed. 'I'll be with him at all times,' she reassured me. 'Thank you,' I replied. I didn't know what else to say. I couldn't think straight. I felt hot and ill, like I needed to be sick. I steadied myself with the side of the bed as best I could. And then I felt it begin to bubble in the pit of my stomach. Rage. Someone had done this to Seán. This wasn't an accident. This was someone's fault. He looked so lifeless, so vulnerable and so sick. How could one human being do this to another? It made no sense to me.

By the time Peter Moore had made it back to his seat, Liverpool were well ahead of Roma. They had scored five times in the opening 68 minutes, but Peter had missed all of the goals. Liverpool manager Jürgen Klopp decided to rest Mo Salah, who had netted twice against his old club. Following the substitution, things took a turn and Roma gave themselves a chance for the return leg with two late goals. The final score was a 5–2 victory for the Reds. Afterwards manager Jürgen Klopp and the players were briefed on what had happened to Seán. One of the players, Alex Oxlade-Chamberlain, had suffered a serious knee injury during the match. It would rule the midfielder out of England's World Cup squad, the Champions League Final and virtually all of Liverpool's following season. But despite his own disappointment, he put a message of support on social media for Seán the following morning. 'This all pales in comparison to how the family of the Liverpool fan badly hurt before last night's game must be feeling,' he tweeted. Peter later told me the result of what began as such an important game for Liverpool was immaterial in the end.

One of their fans had been critically injured, and no one knew if he was going to survive.

17 Seconds

Over the next few hours different parts of the jigsaw were pieced together. Detective Inspector Paul Speight of Merseyside Police came to see me at The Walton Centre, accompanied by a woman called Lisa Hurst who was a family liaison officer. Inspector Speight was leading the investigation into the assault on Seán. He offered me his sympathies and explained that a team of police officers had already been assigned to the case. Suddenly all the questions that had been whirling around my head were being answered and the story took shape. Seán and Marty had been walking up Walton Breck Road just outside Anfield stadium when they were surrounded by a group of up to 60 Roma fans. DI Speight explained this wasn't a group of ordinary football fans like Seán and Marty and the thousands of others making their way into Anfield. This was a group of organised hooligans who had travelled to Liverpool to cause trouble. They were wearing dark clothes and had their faces covered by balaclavas. Some of them were carrying belts with ornate buckles on them. As the chanting grew louder Marty turned to Seán to signal it was time to get out of there, but it was too late. Seán had been hit in the side of the head and was unconscious before he hit the ground, his Liverpool FC scarf lying beside him.

The attack was completely unprovoked and had lasted 17 seconds. I couldn't get my head around it; 17 seconds was all it took to change a life forever. Marty had dropped to his knees to help Seán, but he was out cold. He placed his own body over Seán's to try to protect him. Suddenly I realised the enormity of what Marty had been through. The two brothers had been laughing as they walked up the road, soaking in the atmosphere, feeling like the luckiest pair in the world. Their only care in that moment was that Liverpool would come away with a win. And then the unthinkable happened. Marty had sat in the waiting room all night while Seán was in surgery. A nurse had made him some toast, but he couldn't eat it. At around 5 a.m. he had been brought into the ICU to see Seán. He couldn't believe what had happened. I knew from the way that Marty had looked at me earlier that morning in the waiting room that he felt some sort of responsibility for it. He was the one who had secured the tickets, at the last minute. If he hadn't, they wouldn't have been there in the first place. It was a stroke of 'luck' that could prove fatal for Seán. But I never saw it that way. As far as I was concerned, it could have just as easily been Marty lying in a bed in intensive care fighting for his life.

DI Speight continued to outline the events of the previous night. Inside Anfield's operations room the club's crisis protocol had kicked in. Merseyside Police were given access to the stadium's high-definition CCTV system, and investigating officers had spent hours trawling through it.

They had identified two men, who police had now arrested. The liaison officer, Lisa Hurst, stayed in contact with me over the following days to keep me informed about the investigation and to inquire how Seán was doing. Within days there was an update. The CCTV footage had been viewed from different angles and a third man who was involved had been identified. The detectives believed this man had left the scene after the attack, had changed his hoodie and hat and had then entered the stadium to watch the match. They believed he had subsequently left Liverpool and had returned to Italy. They assured me they were doing everything in their power to track him down. I couldn't believe the cruelty of what I was hearing. Attacking someone for no reason, hitting them in the side of the head and leaving them for dead before continuing with your evening and going to watch a match? DI Speight kept his promise and this third man was later tracked down to his home in Rome and arrested.

Meanwhile at Liverpool FC, efforts were being made to find out more about the fan who had been so horribly injured. How was he doing? Who had been with him? What could be done for his family? A decision was made to contact me. Later that day Tony Barrett, Liverpool's head of club and supporter liaison, and the club's chaplain, a man called Bill Bygroves, arrived at The Walton Centre to see me. The club was shocked and appalled over what had happened to Seán. Tony Barrett assured me Liverpool FC was there to support us in whatever way it could. Before he left, he gave me the contact details for Lisa Rigby, who is a personal assistant at the club. Tony said Lisa would help us with the logistics of getting the children to Liverpool to see Seán over the coming days. If we contacted her, she would book any flights and accommodation needed for the family. I was still in shock. I felt like I had completely lost control of everything and was just being carried along on a wave, so it was a relief to know we could pass those practicalities over to someone else. By the time that first day in The Walton Centre came to an end, I knew if Seán survived the night we were in this for the long haul. Professor Eldridge and his team did not mince their words about the situation. They were taking Seán's condition hour by hour and at any point things could change. Patience was the order of the day – a lot of patience. Seán had come through the surgery, but this was only the very beginning.

After my meetings with DI Speight and Tony Barrett, I returned to the side of Seán's bed in the ICU. I looked around at the other patients and their families, struck by the fact that we weren't the only ones in this desperate situation. The ICU was full of gravely ill people, and as I sat and listened to the beeping of the machines, I knew that some would make it out and others sadly wouldn't. I knew I had to stay positive. 'Seán is fit and healthy and strong,' I told myself. And it was true. Seán was probably in the best shape of his life just before he was attacked. I thought back to the previous Christmas when he had booked himself in for a routine check-up with the doctor. He hadn't liked the results. Seán's cholesterol was high, and the doctor told him he was borderline diabetic. He needed to lose two stone in weight. I still remember the day he arrived back at the house after his appointment. He was raging with himself for not being on top of his health. It was exactly two weeks before Christmas Day so I presumed he would enjoy the festive season and then on the 1 January set about undertaking a cleaner, healthier regime. That is what most people would have done, but not Seán. Immediately he cut back on his portion sizes, he had very little alcohol to drink over Christmas and he started running and cycling. Before long he had shifted exactly two stone. I laughed as I remembered him marching back to tell the doctor the good news.

Since the beginning of the New Year he had continued to eat healthily and exercise regularly. And just two days before going to Liverpool he had completed the KBC Dublin Night Run with his cousin Richard Smith. He had raved about the atmosphere as thousands of people pounded the streets of Dublin city centre at nighttime. Both Seán and Richard got such a high from running with a crowd they signed themselves up to do the Dublin Marathon later in the year. The last photograph taken of Seán before the attack was from the night of the run. Richard's wife, Una, was great at taking pictures and as Seán and Richard made their way back to the car park, tired but thrilled after the run, she asked them to pose with their medals. 'Not another one!' they protested, but she insisted. I couldn't count the amount of times I've looked at that photograph since. Seán was fit and strong and healthy, and had no underlying medical issues – surely this was something to be positive about? But Professor Eldridge's parting words rang in my ears. 'Seán may not survive the night. He may not make it.' But I had to have hope. If I didn't, I had nothing.

Bad News Travels Fast

I needed to talk to Jack, Shauna and Emma. I was so worried about them, and I needed them to know what was going on. Their dad was fighting for his life in intensive care and their mam had disappeared to be by his side. They were all on their own, waiting for news. I had to fill them in as best I could and I felt I owed it to them to be completely honest. Months later I remember someone saying to me that I was lucky they weren't younger at the time of the attack. I didn't see it that way, though. They were still young; Jack, the eldest, was 20, Shauna was 19 and Emma, the youngest, was 16. Emma went to school that first morning – I think she needed the distraction. They all knew it was going to be hours before I'd have any news to tell them and she didn't want to wait around the house all day, so she got up and got ready for school. Emma never ate breakfast, so every morning before school Seán made her a smoothie to give her some energy until lunchtime. The deal was he drank half of it and Emma drank the other half and he wouldn't let her out the door until she finished it. Seán had gotten up before everyone else the morning he left for his early flight to Liverpool, but he didn't forget the smoothie. He had his half before heading for the airport and Emma's half was in the fridge with her name on it. I can't imagine what it was like for her heading off to school without her usual smoothie on board, and not knowing how her Dad was, but I guess it was her way of coping. Jack and Shauna waited at the house for me to call. Some of my family and Seán's family had joined them and their friends had called too to support them. They all knew Seán. 'It's your dad, he's strong and healthy and fit – he's going to be fine,' they tried to reassure them.

I rang home and spoke to Jack and Shauna. I was glad Emma wasn't there at the time as I wasn't sure how they were going to react to the news. I explained that their dad's brain had been injured and there was a lot of swelling, but that he had made it through the surgery. I didn't conceal the fact that we didn't know how this was going to go. 'The next few days are going to be tough,' I warned them. They were completely shocked and devastated. They were also angry that someone had done this to their beloved dad. I told them we were going to make some plans to get them to Liverpool to see their dad as soon as we could. I needed them to see him in case the worst was going to happen. They broke the news to Emma when she came home from school. Apart from the time Seán and I had gone on the cruise to celebrate our wedding anniversary they had never been on their own, and even then they had family checking in on them. I was so anxious that they were in Dunboyne and I was in Liverpool. I remember the relief I felt after I spoke to them. It was true that their mam and dad weren't there with them, but they weren't alone. They had been taken into the arms of our extended family and close friends. Our neighbours Susan and Claire were making sure they had everything they needed. Another one of our neighbours, Constance, even offered to do the ironing for them. People were so kind, and the children were never on their own.

At this stage the news about the attack on Seán had circulated around the village of Dunboyne and further afield. It was being reported on the news and a camera crew from RTÉ had camped on the village green. A newspaper reporter knocked on our door and asked Jack to comment on what had happened. People were really shocked. Seán was well known in our local community. He was not only involved in the GAA; we were also part of the local athletics club and he played golf. He had a wide circle of friends and was universally liked and respected. Everyone was finding it hard to process what had happened. The previous night I had taken a call from a good friend of Seán's, Fergus McNulty, who was the chairman of St Peter's GAA Club at the time. Fergus and his family live in the housing estate opposite us and himself and Seán had gotten to know one another through their involvement with the club. Seán had a close association with Round Tower GAA Club in Clondalkin and Fergus with Lucan Sarsfields so when the two met at St Peter's they hit it off. What began as a working relationship had quickly developed into a friendship. He was shocked to hear what had happened and assured me the club was there to offer whatever support and help we needed. Members of our local community were going above and beyond the call of duty to show their support. 'It's like a food mountain,' said Jack during one of those early conversations. 'The food just keeps on coming.' Emma's friends came to see her and they thought that caterers had been in the house when they saw the boxes of food lining the counter tops and filling the fridge. People were doing what Irish people always do at a time of crisis: they were making sure no one was hungry. They showed their kindness through dinners and cakes which were dropped to the house for the children. They were well looked after but it was so tough on them.

The GAA club was being inundated with calls, either from media outlets looking for a comment or from people offering their support. Fergus stayed in touch with me over the following days and eventually we made the decision that the club should issue a short statement: 'Seán is a long-serving and popular member of St Peter's GAA Club in Dunboyne. At this point we hope that Seán is receiving all of the medical care he requires and that he makes a full and speedy recovery.' Fergus and I didn't know each other well but he knew from Seán that I am a very private person. The statement went on to say, 'Our thoughts and prayers are with Seán and his family and we hope they get the privacy and space they need. We will not be making any further statement at this time.' A few days later Fergus called me to ask my permission for a mass to be held in Dunboyne to pray for Seán's recovery. He told me that everyone was in shock and at a loss to know what the right thing to do was. I agreed. Hundreds of people packed into St Peter and Paul's church in Dunboyne to show their support. I rang Jack afterwards and he was upset. 'It's like he's dead!' he said. I felt so upset for them. Initially when I asked the children about it they thought Seán would just be mentioned during the mass. But when they arrived, they were brought up to the front row and the whole mass was dedicated to Seán. When they left the church there were cameras outside. I explained to him that when tragedy hits a close community like Dunboyne, people don't know what to do. They want to help but they don't know how to, so they often come together to pray. Coming together in one place like that gave people a feeling of closeness. The children understood that people meant well but it was just so hard on all of them. The truth of the matter was at that stage many people feared Seán would die. People knew that the next few days were going to be critical for him, and that he might not make it. I remember Fergus telling me much later that on one of those very early days he had been driving by the GAA club when he noticed that the flag masts in the grounds were crooked, from general wear and tear. He pulled over, called one of the groundsmen and told him they'd have to be straightened immediately. Fergus was preparing for the worst to happen. You couldn't fly a flag at half-mast on a crooked post. Out of respect for Seán and everything he had given to the club, he wasn't going to allow that to happen. I couldn't help but think back on the time many years before when Seán had convinced me to move to Dunboyne. 'This is a real community,' he'd said to me. 'This is where we want to live and rear the kids.' And how right he was.

Home from Home

I knew I was going to be in Liverpool with Seán for the foreseeable future, so I had to make some plans, sort out the logistics. The Walton Centre informed me that I could avail of accommodation they had on-site for families. 'Home from Home' was situated at the back of the hospital and was only a six-minute walk from Seán's bedside. It was available to the families of patients who lived too far away to go home each day. It had several bedrooms, bathrooms, a communal kitchen and dining area and a place where you could do your laundry. It was a godsend. It meant I could spend all of my time with Seán and I'd only have to walk the short distance back there at night. Marty had made his way back to Dublin at this stage. He wasn't physically injured but he was traumatised by what had happened. I knew how hard that journey home was going to be for him. Touching down on Irish soil on his own, without his brother. I know he felt like he had left Seán behind, but we had encouraged him to go. I knew he needed to be with his wife, Ruth, and his family.

Seán's brother Peter stayed with me as we began to navigate this new strange reality. Those very early days are a blur. Work made contact to let me know that everyone was thinking of me and praying for Seán. Some days I was like a headless chicken, trying to come to terms with what had happened. Other days I was calm, as I sat and just watched Seán sleeping. The days all merged together. Each one felt like a month long. I got up every morning and had my breakfast with Peter before walking over to the ICU to see Seán. The nurses would fill us in on how he had been during the night. He was in an induced coma so most days they didn't have much to report but they always tried to impart some little detail about how he had been when I wasn't with him; I think they knew how important that was to me. Seán was stable but heavily sedated. My days were spent sitting with him holding his hand. Sometimes I'd just pray and pray that he would survive. Sometimes all I could do was cry. My mind was working overtime. 'Am I going to be a widow?' I'd think to myself before trying my best to push the thought from my mind. I had heard somewhere before that when people are in a coma, they can sometimes hear what's going on around them. I didn't know if it was true, but I didn't know it wasn't. So, I talked to Seán a lot. I'd tell him what I had done that morning, what day it was. Sometimes I'd tell him more. After a few hours I'd take a break to have something to eat, and Peter would sit with him. The Home from Home didn't have a cooker but it had a microwave and a fridge, so I'd walk back there and have some lunch. I got to know the families of the other patients in ICU. We'd sometimes sit and have a cup of tea and a chat. I guess we all had something in common. I'd then return to Seán's bedside to continue the waiting game. The hours and days went on like that. There was still so much uncertainty; the doctors didn't know if Seán would survive.

After a few days Peter went home, and Seán's first cousin Richard came to Liverpool. Both of our families showed us enormous support in those early days. Watching Seán lying helpless in his hospital bed made me feel incredibly lonely. I missed him so much, but I always had someone with me at The Walton Centre. I look back on that now and realise how lucky I was to have that support. I don't know what I would have done without it. After a few days we made some plans for the kids to travel to Liverpool. Even at this early stage all three of them were coping in different ways. Jack was reluctant to come over. I think he feared that once he saw Seán with his own two eyes the reality of what had happened would hit him. Shauna was the opposite and wanted to get on a flight straight away. I was particularly worried about Emma, and I felt it might be too much for her to see her dad in such a bad way. We agreed that the children would come separately: Shauna would come over to Liverpool first while Jack stayed at home with Emma, then when Shauna went home Jack could come out.

Seán's sister Suzanne and Shauna travelled together. I felt such relief at seeing their faces, but I was so anxious about them seeing Seán, especially Shauna. I tried my best to prepare them both, but I knew nothing I could say would limit the shock they were both going to get. 'He doesn't look like himself,' I warned them before we entered the ICU. 'He has a lot of tubes and machines around him, and his head is very swollen.' Shauna later told me she had a *Grey's Anatomy* image in her head of what she was going to see. But when she saw her dad there was nothing fictional about it. She broke down as I pulled the curtain around Seán for some privacy. The enormity of his injuries hit her like a ton of bricks. She was just so heartbroken over how helpless he was. He had always been her big, strong, healthy dad and now he was anything but. He looked so vulnerable.

Jack was terribly nervous when his turn came to travel to The Walton Centre to visit his dad. We were both shaking as we waited outside the ICU to go in. Just like me, he felt sick when he saw how badly injured Seán was – he couldn't believe that it was his dad in the bed. He just sat by his side and cried. It was heartbreaking to watch. He didn't tell me at the time, because he was trying to stay strong for me, but he didn't think Seán would survive. And I can understand why. Seán looked so injured and damaged it was hard to imagine him pulling through. By the time Emma arrived in Liverpool I hadn't seen her in almost three weeks. We had never been apart for that long. I knew she hated hospitals, so I brought her to where we were staying first. Eventually we made our way over to the hospital. I remember how shaky she was as we walked down the long corridor to the double doors of the ICU. She had no idea what was behind those doors. I asked the nurses to pull the curtain around Seán's bed to give us some privacy. But she surprised us all and began talking to her dad as soon as she saw him. She told me afterwards she didn't think there was any point in freaking out; it wasn't going to help anyone. All three of them showed such bravery in those early days. Each one of them sat with Seán for hours, talking to him, telling him what was going on. They hugged him and kissed him and rubbed his hands.

We had no idea if Seán was taking any of this in. He was still heavily sedated, breathing with the help of a ventilator. We stayed by his bedside. He hadn't moved a muscle or opened his eyes, but we all hoped he would. We all acted like it was going to happen, any day now, any minute.

King Kenny's Cappuccino

As April came to an end and a new month began, Seán's medical team was hoping to begin the process of waking Seán up. This was the next step; it was what needed to happen to provide us with more information. His doctors were describing his brain injury as 'profound' but I didn't really know what that meant. Everything moved very slowly, there was a lot of second-guessing, but Seán needed to be awake for us to find out just how badly injured he was. We set up a WhatsApp group to help us communicate everything that was happening in Liverpool with our family and close friends at home. We called it 'Seán's Recovery' and as the days went on we used it as a way of planning visits by different family members. Seán's sisters and brothers came to visit as did mine, along with some of our close friends. Waking Seán up involved very slowly weaning him off the ventilator which was helping him to breathe. We wouldn't know if he could breathe on his own until they attempted this. One message into the group read, 'Spoke to Professor Eldridge earlier this morning, thankfully Seán's swelling has decreased, and Tuesday is still the day they hope to be able to start the process of waking Seán.' The next day Jack posted, 'Another stable night for Dad, comfortable and strong, which is what we need, another day closer.' My good friend Denise, who I knew from working at Dunnes Stores, also came to Liverpool to see Seán and to support me. 'Hi all, Denise here, I'm with Martina and Jack today, the doctors scanned Seán, they are going to start withdrawing sedation and insert a tracheostomy to help Seán's breathing, as we all know withdrawing sedation can take days so we will let you all know how it goes.' The messages continued day in, day out as we waited for something to happen.

One entry, posted 5 May 2018 by Richard, stands out. It was a photograph of a Liverpool jersey with the caption, 'Present from King Kenny for Seán, a true gent'. A few days before, Tony Barrett from Liverpool FC had contacted me to say that Kenny Dalglish wanted to visit me to offer his support. I know very little about soccer in general or about the history of Liverpool, but I didn't spend 30 years of my life with Seán and not take some of it in. Kenny Dalglish was a legend of the game of football. Jack filled in the gaps for me. He was a former player and manager at Liverpool and Glasgow Celtic. He had been capped over a hundred times for Scotland and had scored 172 times during his time at Liverpool. He was one of Seán's sporting heroes. I knew he had been knighted for his role in advocating for the victims of the Hillsborough disaster in 1989, which had claimed the lives of 96 people. He was certainly royalty in this area. I agreed to meet him, but I wanted to do so privately – I was sure people would recognise him at the hospital and I didn't want there to be any fuss, so we arranged to meet at the Home from Home accommodation, which was much quieter. Jack and Richard were in Liverpool at the time visiting Seán so the three of us made our way to a little café at the side of the accommodation. He pulled up outside and came in to greet us. We had just introduced ourselves when the girl working behind the counter spotted him and went into a tailspin. She ran over to the table. 'What can I get you, Kenny?' she asked, ignoring the rest of us. He ordered a cappuccino and waited for her to take our order, but she just ran back behind the counter to get his coffee. We all started laughing. What an ice-breaker! Our quiet, private coffee didn't go to plan. Nearly everyone who walked by recognised him, people stopped to say hello and some of them even asked for photographs. Despite the interruptions we spent about an hour with him. He told us how sorry he was about what had happened to Seán. He said he was disgusted at the brutality of the attack and that he was there to support us and Seán in any way he could. Before we parted, he gave me one of his jerseys for Seán, which I found really touching. I felt he was personally very troubled by what had happened and his concern for Seán and for us as a family was very genuine. It wasn't the only jersey that had exchanged hands. Liverpool FC had asked for a St Peter's GAA jersey to hang in the players' dressing room in Anfield in honour of Seán. Fergus McNulty from the club had flown over to see Seán and had brought one with him, travelling to Anfield to hand it over. It was hung beside Mo Salah's shirt ahead of Liverpool's Premier League match with Stoke City a few days later. Liverpool FC manager Jürgen Klopp gave a press conference before the match. Wearing a tricolour badge, he said what had happened to Seán 'should never have happened and highlighted the ugly side of football'.

A few days later the team travelled to Rome for the second leg of the Champions League Semi-final with Roma. They lost that game, but it didn't matter: they had made it through to the final on aggregate – they had a greater number of goals overall. As the celebrations erupted in the Stadio Olimpico, the captain, Jordan Henderson, paraded a banner around the pitch dedicated to Seán. It was there because of the Liverpool supporters' group, Spirit of Shankly, and two die-hard Reds fans, Stephen Monahan and Peter Carney. Since the seventies Peter has made all the banners that people see on the Kop in Anfield. He was actually a survivor of the Hillsborough disaster. What he saw that day at Hillsborough Stadium in Sheffield stayed with him, and over the years he has campaigned for justice for the victims and their families. Stephen Monahan asked Peter to make a banner for Seán and he agreed. It read 'Seán Cox, You'll Never Walk Alone' but not just in English. He had also written it as Gaeilge and in Italian too. The sentence 'Ní shiúlfaidh tú i d'aonar go deo' was etched across the fabric as a nod to Seán's other love, the GAA. Marty later told me that it had been Peter Carney's birthday in the week running up to the Rome game. He had stayed up all night to finish it, putting a huge amount of work into it. Stephen Monahan then managed to get it to the players just before they flew out to Rome. Those gestures went over my head at the time because all I could do was focus on Seán but sometimes, now, I think back, and I'm amazed at the kindness we were shown.

On 9 May Jack posted another message in the WhatsApp group, 'Nurses are happy with Dad who is now doing some breathing by himself,' followed by an update from Shauna a few days later: 'Just out from Dad, nurses are happy with him and his breathing, he is also responding to some touch, Professor says it's baby steps at the minute, and we need to take it day by day.' We documented every little detail: the first time Seán was put into a sitting position in the bed, the first time he moved his arm ever so slightly, the first time his eyes flickered. They were the smallest milestones but at the time they were massive. We had come from a place of thinking Seán might not make it so each tiny development took on huge significance for us and for our close circle, who were receiving the messages at home. I sometimes look back on those WhatsApp messages from Seán's time in The Walton Centre. On the bad days they remind me of how far he has come. Some of them are harder to read than others. One update from Shauna read, 'Dad off the ventilator for four hours last night, going good, Mr Stubborn hasn't opened his eyes yet.' A few days later Emma let everyone know that Seán was having a sleepy day: 'Dad tired today, overdid it yesterday, he did try to open his eyes, tomorrow is another day.' That in a way sums up how we ended each day at The Walton Centre. Hoping tomorrow would bring something more.

Seán's mini milestones, as I called them, were not only recorded in our 'Seán's Recovery' WhatsApp group. The Walton Centre had given us a patient diary to fill in for Seán every day. It was a way of tracking his progress over the course of his stay there. You don't get the diary back when you leave the centre; the whole idea behind it is you come back and collect it when you've recovered. It's a way of documenting how far a patient comes over several weeks or months or years, depending on how severe the person's condition is. Every ICU patient has one and before long filling it out became part of our daily routine. Whoever was there on a given day would take responsibility for filling in the diary: what day it was, what the weather was like and who had been visiting. They'd also give a little synopsis of how Seán had been that day. The nurses also added little notes, detailing how Seán had slept, if he wiggled his toes or moved his arm. Jack was particularly dedicated to filling out Seán's patient diary. He found talking to Seán when he was still unconscious difficult. I totally understood – it's hard to chat to someone who is asleep, when it's all one way and you're not getting anything back. Sometimes it can make you feel like you're losing your mind. He sat with his dad for hours on end and then wrote his thoughts into the diary. Just over a week after the attack it was Jack's birthday. He was turning 21. That evening he wrote, 'Hi Dad. Today is my birthday. I am 21. Me, Mam and Richard are going to Nando's tonight for dinner.' A milestone birthday for our first-born, one Seán and I had been really looking forward to celebrating. Our oldest child turning 21 felt like such a big deal. We had reminisced about the day in Ballycullen when we found out I was pregnant. I was nervous after my previous miscarriage, but we had been so excited. Seán and I had talked about what we would give Jack for his 21st birthday but here I was in Liverpool with nothing organised for him. I was afraid he'd be disappointed so before he travelled to

Liverpool I sent a text to his girlfriend, Laura, to make sure he knew I didn't have anything planned for him. We would have to hold off on the celebrations. Of course there was no need for the text; Jack knew everything was different now. We had been planning a big fancy family dinner in Fire, the restaurant in the Mansion House in Dublin. Jack had been really looking forward to it. But here he was about to leave his dad's bedside in intensive care and head to Nando's with his mam and his dad's cousin. It was almost too much for me to handle.

A Sixth Sense

As the weeks in May went by, we were approaching the one-month mark of Seán being in intensive care at The Walton Centre. Nearly one full month. If someone told me it had been a year, I would have believed them. At times it felt like time was standing still, though. Long days sitting by Seán's bedside hoping for something to happen. I spent so much of my time just holding his hand. He was still unconscious. Was it possible for someone to be asleep for almost a full month and wake up and recover? I never answered my own questions. I was too afraid to. I'd never had so much time to think. Sitting in the ICU my mind wandered back to different times in the past, all the good times we had shared over the years. There had been so many. Memories that made me laugh and cry at once. On one of those May days as I walked across to be with Seán the morning sun was rising in the sky. Suddenly I thought about Portugal. Our flights had been booked to travel over to close the deal on the apartment, our new home away from home. The thought stopped me in my tracks. Life had changed so completely in such a short space of time, it was hard to comprehend. I had swapped our home away from home for my stay in the Home from Home while Seán fought for his life in hospital.

But it was more than that. After we had paid the deposit on the apartment in Lagos back in February, I had started to buy a few bits and pieces for it. If I was shopping and I saw nice bed linen or towels I'd pick them up for Portugal. Oddly, though, every time I did it, I got this really weird feeling. It's so hard to explain but it just felt wrong. I never told anyone about it because it confused me. Buying a place in Portugal had been a dream of ours for years and we had come to the stage of making that dream a reality. So this weird feeling made no sense at all. It just didn't feel right, like we had made a mistake. I told myself not to be silly and kept my feelings to myself. But as I reached the front door of The Walton Centre I wondered if it had been a sixth sense. Did I even believe in such a thing? The dream holiday apartment certainly wouldn't be happening now, and I made a mental note to contact our solicitor in Portugal. Seán still hadn't opened his eyes. There had been little flickers but nothing to write home about, even though we did just that all the time on the WhatsApp group. At times we were really clutching at straws. I searched and searched for things to be positive about. I knew I had to hold on to some hope that Seán would wake up. Some days were good, and we could see light at the end of the tunnel; on other days we felt deflated. I knew Seán's doctors were hoping for more progress and I had to constantly remind myself to be patient. This was the waiting game we had been told to expect from the very first day.

One of the evenings, myself and Emma, were sitting with Seán. Richard's wife, Una, had travelled to Liverpool to see Seán. We always tried to keep the number of people around Seán's bed to a minimum as I always felt it wasn't fair on the other patients and families in the ICU. It was a gorgeous sunny evening, so Emma and I decided to go have a coffee in the little courtyard at the side of the hospital to allow Richard and Una to have some time with Seán. We were sitting chatting and enjoying the fresh air when the peace was suddenly interrupted by a scream. I looked up to my left to see Richard running like a mad man towards us. 'He's opened his eyes, come on quick!' he shouted. Emma and I jumped out of our seats and started to run. There was tight security around the unit with codes for each door to prevent anyone from entering who wasn't supposed to be there. Richard held the doors open for us as we ran to get to Seán. A few days before when Seán's sister Sinéad had been visiting, Seán had briefly opened his eyes but closed them again. 'They'll be closed again,' I shouted at Emma as we ran to the ICU. When we arrived, breathless, there he was lying in the bed with his eyes open. It genuinely felt like we had won the Lotto. Emma started to cry, and I told her to stop. I didn't want Seán to see any of us upset. This is what we had been waiting for. He wasn't fully focused on us, but this was a significant development. For more than a month now we had sat at the side of his bed willing him to wake up. He did it! This was the start, as before there had been nothing. It felt like a massive win. I rang Jack to tell him and I think it was the first time he allowed himself to believe that his dad was going to make it. That night we went to Nando's for our dinner to celebrate and Emma updated the 'Seán's Recovery' WhatsApp group: 'Hi all, a great evening with Dad, he opened his eyes for 35 minutes, he was blinking and moving his eyes from left to right.' The following morning brought more good news: 'Dad awake when we went in to see him this morning, eyes open again and breathing on his own for a full 24 hours – brilliant progress.' Everyone was thrilled and hugely relieved. Our families and close friends had spent the previous month willing Seán along; everyone had played their part. It was such a wonderful feeling to be able to share some positive news with them.

It was at this point that the wheels were put in motion to bring Seán back to Dublin. Professor Eldridge at The Walton Centre had been in contact with Beaumont Hospital and before long a neurologist there agreed to take on Seán's case. He would be under the care of Mr Mohsen Javadpour. On 25 May Jack delivered the news everyone had been waiting for, 'We're coming home. Dad is going on a flight tomorrow.' Everyone was delighted but I was terrified. I knew Seán had a massive mountain to climb and I was worried about moving him. To the outside world getting Seán home was a massive milestone – it was what we were working towards – but I was scared about the road ahead. I felt cocooned in Liverpool and it was extremely hard to say goodbye. Professor Eldridge and his team had saved Seán's life. The nurses in the intensive care unit had cared for him like he was a member of their own family. Seán had received one-to-one nursing care for the past four and a half weeks. But now the time had come to begin the next chapter. I had spent the previous month wishing and hoping for something to happen and now it felt like everything was happening too quickly. Our plans were put in place; we would be brought by ambulance to the airport where Seán would be placed in an air ambulance. I could travel with him. On arrival in Dublin Airport we would be met by an ambulance from Beaumont Hospital. As Seán was wheeled out of The Walton Centre on a stretcher I broke down. It was like going back to the very first day when myself and Peter had arrived from Dublin. Seán suddenly looked so ill and so helpless all over again. He still wasn't fully conscious and seeing him outside the safety of the ICU made him seem even more vulnerable. I was heartbroken. I still didn't know if I believed in such a thing as a sixth sense, but something was telling me if things were going to get better, they were going to get worse first.

Beaumont Hospital

Being back on Irish soil was very strange. I had left Dublin with Peter on that early Wednesday morning flight to Liverpool almost five weeks ago to be with Seán. I thought back to being on the plane, unable to stomach a cup of coffee. I had no idea then what was ahead of me. Since then I had barely left Seán's bedside. I had entered a world I never thought I'd have to be a part of. To those on the outside it was fantastic that Seán had made it back to Dublin, and of course it was a massive milestone for him and for us as a family. But our lives had changed completely. I was back in my own bed, but I was without Seán. What had happened almost seemed more real now. I knew I had to mind Seán and make sure he was given the best chance of recovery, but it was hard. I felt like I'd done a crash course in medicine over the past month. I was getting familiar with terms I had never heard before and could barely pronounce. I felt a huge amount of responsibility to keep on top of Seán's care, to ask the right questions and to make the right decisions. He could not speak for himself anymore. I was now his voice, and it scared me.

We arrived back in Dublin still so uncertain about Seán's injury. The questions far outweighed the answers. Every injury to a brain, I had learned, is completely unique and as a result predicting how someone may or may not recover is extremely difficult. I often thought about Professor Eldridge's blunt warning on the first day I met him at The Walton Centre. 'Seán's injuries are life-changing,' he had said. Everyone was in agreement that his injury was what's described as 'profound' but what exactly that meant for Seán and for us as a family no one could really tell me. For example, I didn't know if Seán would walk or talk again. Would he know us? Would he be able to communicate with us? Would he sit up, eat, drink? There were no definitive answers so I did the only thing I could do. I stopped speculating about what 'better' looked like for Seán. In many ways I didn't really want to know the answer. I decided the only way forward was to take one day at a time. Our flight back to Dublin Airport in the air ambulance had gone well and we landed safely. We were met by a team from Beaumont who took us to the hospital where Seán was taken straight through to the intensive care unit to be settled. Before long I was brought in to see him. As soon as I entered the ICU I was struck by how different it was to where we had just come from. It seemed smaller and much busier than The Walton Centre. There were a lot of people coming and going and very little space between each patient. Seán had been settled into his bed and he seemed very comfortable, so I put any worries out of my head. The past 24 hours had been stressful. Finding out Seán was being transferred to Dublin had happened really quickly and I had found the flight home really surreal and emotional. It's just one of those things you hope you'll never have to do: take a trip in an air ambulance. I was exhausted and I knew it was going to take a few days for me to get used to our new surroundings. I hadn't even thought yet about the logistics of Seán being in Beaumont – what the visiting times were and where I'd park. My six-minute walk from the Home from Home accommodation in Liverpool was about to become a 50-kilometre daily round trip on Ireland's busiest motorway, the M50. Once Seán continued to recover, I knew I'd manage whatever I had to.

The doctors assessed Seán when he arrived in the intensive care unit and he was moved to a high dependency unit where he stayed for a few weeks. We were then surprised to hear he was being moved to a unit described as 'low dependency'. To a stranger I am sure this would have sounded like positive news, an indicator of Seán's progress, but to anyone who had spent any amount of time with Seán over the past few weeks, it caused alarm bells to ring. Seán was gravely ill but there was someone who was sicker, and they needed the bed. He still spent most of the day asleep with only small periods when his eyes were open. His tracheostomy was still in place, which was helping him with his breathing, and he had a nasogastric feeding tube. We had no idea how much of what was going on around him he was taking in. His nursing needs were substantial. The ratio of nurses to patients in this low dependency unit was six to one. Seán was going from having one-to-one care in The Walton Centre to sharing a nurse with five other patients. I was really concerned. That first morning when he was moved to the low dependency unit, I walked in to find that he had been placed in the bed at the far end of the ward, the bed farthest away from the nurse's station. I rang a friend of mine who is a nurse to ask her advice. 'I'm really worried something will go wrong for Seán and he won't be able to alert anyone, he's hidden away, and he can't call for help,' I said to her on the phone. She told me it didn't seem right that someone so vulnerable would be positioned at the far end of the ward and she advised me to mention it to the head nurse. I didn't want to make a fuss: the hospital was busy, and the doctors, nurses and healthcare staff all seemed under pressure. But I also knew that I could not live with myself if something happened to Seán. I had to speak up on his behalf. I had to make sure he was getting the care he needed and deserved.

The next day I brought it up with the head nurse. She listened to my concerns and told me I had nothing to worry about. I filed it away in the back of my head, hoping I wouldn't have to return to it. Before we had left The Walton Centre, Professor Eldridge had stressed the importance of ensuring Seán got as much rehabilitation as he could manage. 'The more rehab he gets, the better his chances are,' he had said. One of my first jobs back in Dublin was to set those wheels in motion. We didn't know how long Seán was going to be a patient at Beaumont for. He had opened his eyes and there were small signs he was becoming more alert as the weeks passed but what the future held was still anyone's guess. I was still following my own advice to not think too far down the line but at times I couldn't help but wonder. Will I see him walk again? Will I hear him laugh? Will I see him smile? One thing I did know for sure was that I would do everything in my power to help Seán along the way. I also knew I couldn't do it on my own, so I did what I had done when Seán was admitted to The Walton Centre: I called in the troops. Our family and close friends would help me to help Seán.

We set up a rota of people who could visit Seán: Jack, Shauna and Emma; Seán's sisters, Sinéad and Suzanne; his brothers, Peter and Marty; my family; and, of course, some of our close friends who had been such a massive support to us. Seán was never short of visitors. One of the days Shauna and Emma went in to spend some time with their dad. When they left, they reported that he had been sleepy but comfortable, which was good news, but both of them came away from the hospital upset. Since Seán had been attacked, he had been wearing a hospital gown, at first in Liverpool and then in Beaumont. He had been too ill to be put through the ordeal of dressing him in anything else, so he had stayed in a hospital gown. A few days before the girls' visit a nurse on his ward told me that if I brought in clothes for Seán, they'd start dressing him and getting him out of the gowns. I was delighted as it felt like a bit of progress, so off I went and gathered numerous pairs of comfortable shorts and T-shirts and packed them away beside his bed. But that night when the girls arrived to see their dad, he had been lying there with no shorts on, fully exposed. It really upset them. They didn't want to see him like that with no dignity in a busy hospital ward with people coming and going. And neither did I. From the minute I'd first seen Seán lying in that bed in The Walton Centre I had such a ferocious urge to always protect his privacy. I knew it would be important to him. Even though Seán was sociable, deep down he was very reserved and at times shy. He was a private person. The idea of him being stripped of his dignity was too much for me. I brought this up with the head nurse, explaining I really didn't want it to happen again. I wanted Seán's privacy to be respected. It was the least we could do for him now. Again, I was told I had nothing to worry about and in future Seán would be fully dressed.

Most days I visited Seán twice. I liked to go in to see him in the early afternoon and then go home to Dunboyne for an hour or two before going back in to say goodnight to him. It was so different from when I had been living in Liverpool. I wanted to try to get back some sense of our old life. I felt the need to cook a dinner or do the laundry, keep things ticking over in the house. I wanted to be there for Jack, Shauna and Emma. I knew they were all struggling in their own ways to come to terms with what had happened so I wanted to give them back a little bit of normality. At the end of the summer Jack and Shauna would be returning to college and Emma would be starting her final year of secondary school. I wanted to make sure they were all doing okay. But there was so much going on in my head. One day I arrived home to notice my bins hadn't been collected. They were full and I was raging as I needed them emptied. I rang the waste disposal company, braced to tell them what I thought of their service. 'You haven't paid your charges, Mrs Cox,' the man explained on the phone. The reminder had been sent to Seán's email.

Travelling from Dunboyne to Beaumont twice a day was tough going. Some days I'd get stuck on the dreaded M50 on my way home from the hospital, arriving in Dunboyne much later than expected. I might have an hour in the house before I'd turn around and head back to Beaumont. Some weeks I clocked up more than 1,000 kilometres on my car. I also spent an obscene amount of money on the car park. I couldn't believe that there was no special offer for people who had a loved one in hospital for a prolonged period of time. I asked for a pass, which I eventually got months into Seán's stay. I was exhausted. A few days after the incident with Shauna and Emma, I discovered Seán in the same state. The hospital was always warm, so Seán had thrown the sheet off himself and he wasn't wearing any shorts. I couldn't believe it. The nurses had assured me they wouldn't let this happen again. This wasn't a big ask – it was such a simple thing – but it was so important to me because I knew it would be important to Seán. I called the nearest nurse I could find and asked her how this had happened again. Her explanation: they were trying to save my washing. I couldn't believe what I was hearing. Unfortunately, that wasn't the last time I had to have that conversation.

You Don't Even Know
Seán Cox

One of the first goals the medical team at Beaumont Hospital had for Seán was to wean him of his tracheostomy which was still in place when he arrived from The Walton Centre. Thankfully this was a success and it felt like progress. Seán had had this tube in for so many weeks – it was great to see him managing without it. However, his swallow had been compromised as a result. This meant that he often had a lot of fluid in his mouth. It was important that the excess fluid was suctioned away on a regular basis to prevent it from travelling to his chest and causing an infection. I was thrilled that Seán's tracheostomy had been removed, but as soon as it was, I ended up facing another battle over this suctioning process. Some evenings I'd arrive at Seán's bedside to find that his mouth was full of fluid – no one had suctioned him. I'd have to go and ask someone to do it, to take away his discomfort. It was difficult to find him like that. I didn't want to be having tense conversations with people but things like that left me so upset, on Seán's behalf, I just had to speak up.

Some days were harder than others. There was one nurse at Beaumont who caused me huge distress. They were new to the hospital and had only taken up their position shortly before we arrived back from Liverpool. This nurse was responsible for six patients on the ward, including Seán, and as the days and weeks went on, I'd get a pain in the pit of my stomach when I saw that they were on duty. My concerns weren't based on their ability to get the job done, but their manner really bothered me. Over the years I've heard people talk about the importance of a good bedside manner, but I really learned the true value of that during Seán's stay in Beaumont. One day I came in and asked how Seán was doing. I remembered the mornings at The Walton Centre when the nurses would so generously share with me even the tiniest bit of information about how Seán had been during the hours I wasn't with him. On many of those mornings there would have been very little to report as Seán was still in an induced coma, but they always found something to tell me because they knew it was a comfort to me. When you have someone you love in hospital for a long period of time you must accept that you won't always be there. It's just not possible. As a result, you hang on every word of the strangers you leave in charge and great solace can be taken from knowing a comfortable night was had. This particular morning when I asked the nurse in Beaumont how Seán had been, they promptly replied, 'Seán had a large bowel movement,' before quickly walking past me to the next person looking for help. It felt so cold and impersonal. Another day as this nurse was doing their rounds of the patients, they stopped at the side of Seán's bed. It was what we called a sleepy day for Seán, the days where all I could do was sit with him and rub his hand. 'Have you googled Seán's injury?' the nurse asked. I couldn't believe what I was hearing. I'd lost count of the amount of times I'd been warned to never consult Dr Google. The comment felt so inappropriate and tactless. I ended up in front of the head nurse in her office on many occasions. She always assured me she was doing her best. She talked to me about recruitment challenges in the Irish health service and explained that there was very little she could do about the staff being made available to her. But this was no consolation to me.

Seán couldn't speak for himself, and I didn't know if he ever would again. His voice had been taken from him. I had to speak up. I had started to feel really uneasy. It wasn't unusual for me to be anxious and worried about Seán, it was a constant feeling since the moment I heard about the attack, but this felt different. I felt a huge pressure to make sure Seán was getting the care I knew he needed, the care he deserved. 'The more rehab he gets, the better he'll do,' I told myself repeatedly. Seán had been at death's door in The Walton Centre. We were so lucky he had survived those first few critical nights. I always felt he battled hard to stay with us. Now it was my turn to battle for him. I decided to request a meeting with Seán's consultant, Mr Mohsen Javadpour. I asked Seán's sister Sinéad and his cousin Richard to come with me. It was arranged for the following week, but when we arrived at the waiting area, a man I didn't recognise walked in and introduced himself to us. Something had come up for Mr Javadpour so he had sent his registrar. At this stage I had spent my fair share of time in and around hospitals so I knew how extremely busy they can be, but this felt like a slap in the face. I had no relationship with this man standing in front of me and, more importantly, I wasn't confident about how familiar he was with Seán's condition.

He got straight to the point. 'Seán's progress is much slower than we'd like it to be,' he said. I felt like screaming, 'You and me both!' but I stayed quiet. He continued to say the medical team would like to see Seán awake for longer periods and he kept stressing that everything was moving very slowly. There was just a general air of real negativity around the meeting. I was trying to wrap my head around what he was saying but I became really upset and couldn't find any words. Deep down I knew Seán's injury was severe and I understood our lives were never going to be the same again – there was no doubt we had a mountain to climb. I had to hold on to some hope though; if I didn't, I had nothing. It sounded like this man was writing Seán off, putting him on the scrap heap. This wasn't an option for us. Suddenly, Richard was on his feet. Richard is one of the calmest men on the planet, level-headed and always pragmatic, but this was too much for him. 'You don't even know Seán Cox,' he said in a raised voice. Sinéad and I looked at one another. We couldn't believe it. 'And you've made no effort to get to know him,' he continued. 'Yes, he's slow to come around, but he's going to do it, he's a fighter.' The registrar didn't react, and the meeting came to an end. We never ever saw that man again. I am so grateful Richard was with me that day. He managed to articulate exactly what I was thinking. Yes, I was Seán's voice now but at that moment I felt tired and broken. How lucky were we to have Richard to speak for us both that day?

It Takes a Village

That interaction stayed with me for a long time but in a strange way it made me even more determined to make sure Seán got the help he deserved. As the weeks went on in Beaumont Hospital, there were small signs that Seán was becoming more alert. His eyesight had also been damaged in the attack and he had developed a nystagmus flicker, which is quite common in people with brain injuries. The flickering was starting to settle down a bit, but he still had to squint to see things properly. He had started to stay awake for slightly longer periods of time and he'd even wiggled his toes and stuck out his tongue. I knew there was more in there though, I just had to work hard to get it out. I rallied the troops. Through the 'Seán's Recovery' WhatsApp group we established a rota of visitors for Seán, like we had in Liverpool. As before, it included Jack, Shauna and Emma along with Seán's sisters and brothers and our close circle of friends. None of them knew what recovery looked like for Seán but they were more than willing to help get him there. When Seán's mam, Yvonne, had been diagnosed with cancer in 2001, Seán, Peter, Marty, Suzanne and Sinéad had looked after her so well. They had set up a rota and rallied together to make sure everyone was doing their bit, and someone was always with her. Nana Cox or Nana Sweets, as my children always called her, sadly passed away three years later in September 2004. We all missed her so much. The family was determined to do the same for Seán and showed such a level of commitment to do whatever they could for him.

Over the coming weeks our family and close friends came together at Seán's bedside. We constantly talked to him, telling him what day and month it was along with what was going on in the world. We played Liverpool's anthem, 'You'll Never Walk Alone', over and over again, a song he had roared at the top of his lungs thousands of times before. We showed him videos of our two dogs, Roxy and Bruno. We showed him soccer matches and golf tournaments on an iPad. His sister-in-law Aisling did his hair and eyebrows and even his nails. We brought in photo albums and spent hours pointing out the faces of the people he used to know. We rubbed his hands and his arms and his legs. We lay in bed with him and hugged and kissed him. We did anything and everything we could think of to stimulate him. Seán's left-hand side had been badly paralysed in the attack, which was particularly unfortunate as Seán had always been left-handed. So, we began to focus on his right side. We gave him a small ball and encouraged him to squeeze it. We spent hours on end doing the same tasks with him repeatedly. Slowly but surely Seán became more alert and his strength and dexterity started to improve. We still weren't sure if Seán was taking any of this in, but we acted as if he was. He also started to improve medically too. His doctors moved his feeding peg from his nose to his stomach, which was much less invasive.

Then we hit a roadblock. Seán contracted pneumonia and was transferred back into the high dependency unit. I was warned this could prove fatal for Seán, but he battled that too and came out the other side. Then about three weeks into his stay in the unit I arrived in to see him one night. Seán was asleep and his sister Sinéad and cousin Richard were by his bedside. When I said hello to them, Seán opened his eyes and turned his head to look at me. Myself, Sinéad and Richard just froze. Was he really seeing me? I put my hand down on his and he squeezed it. I wasn't sure if I was imagining it; was it a spasm or a fluke? So, I pulled my hand away. I wanted to see how he would react, I needed proof I wasn't imagining it. And then he did it, he grabbed my hand back. He recognised my voice. He knew me. He wanted to hold my hand. These were small but extremely significant milestones. A few evenings later Richard posted in the WhatsApp group, 'Tonight is different as far as I am concerned, I knew instantly when I arrived that Seán knew me, he turned his head and followed me around the bed. And then he smiled, a brilliant smile, I have never been as convinced that he is on his way back.' Everyone was delighted. Seán was ready to come back; we just needed to continue to guide him home.

I had begun to feel frustrated about the level of professional help Seán was receiving in Beaumont. He was making progress with just the help of his family, we were doing all we could, but we were just winging it. What was he capable of in the hands of the right people? Seán did get some physiotherapy and speech and language therapy at Beaumont, but it was minimal. One day as I pulled into the car park of the hospital my mobile phone rang. It was one of Seán's speech therapists. She explained that Seán wasn't engaging with her at all and that she wasn't sure what more she could do with him. I was really taken aback. I told her our experience was the opposite to that; Seán was becoming more alert and seemed to be making progress. I felt like she didn't believe me. I was really upset ending the phone call. I couldn't understand how we couldn't work collaboratively with Seán, both the professional and the personal. I came away thinking she was annoyed with me for trying to help Seán. Did she not realise I had no choice? On other days Seán's physiotherapy and speech and language therapy were scheduled back to back with no break in between, after which I'd be told that Seán wasn't able for it. I knew it would be different if Seán could rest in between each session but it felt like the schedule of therapies was management and staff led, and not patient led. There was no fluidity: the systems were the systems and they had to be followed.

It was a similar situation with a social worker I was put in contact with when Seán was first admitted to Beaumont. At first, she was really helpful in assisting me to sort out Seán's medical card and other insurance forms that needed to be seen to. Once that initial administrative work was completed, though, the social worker seemed to decide that Seán would eventually be going to a nursing home, and she wasn't going to rest until I chose one. It was like this was her mission in life: every time we'd meet, she'd bring it up, reminding me to start looking around for the right nursing home for Seán. I had never ever considered Seán not eventually making it back to our forever home in Dunboyne. And I told her that. She looked at me with pity in her eyes as she handed me the forms for the 'Fair Deal' nursing home scheme. I told her no again. But she wouldn't listen. It wasn't that she even cared where Seán was going to end up: she wanted those forms signed because that was the 'done thing' in this scenario. Protocol and systems followed blindly even when the people at the heart of the decisions were completely against them. Eventually I put my foot down. 'You're not listening to me,' I said. 'You need to stop because Seán isn't going to a nursing home, he's coming home with me.' But even as I stood there finally putting her straight, deep down I didn't really know where Seán was going next. As every day passed, I became more convinced that Seán was in the wrong place. Beaumont Hospital is an acute hospital. Lives are saved there every day of the week and the doctors had looked after Seán's medical needs. But if he was going to begin to climb the mountain he had ahead of him, he needed so much more than that. And he needed it sooner rather than later.

Seán had been assessed to see if he was suitable for a place at the National Rehabilitation Hospital in Dún Laoghaire. I had heard of the NRH over the years and I knew it had an established reputation as a go-to place for brain injury rehabilitation. It offered interdisciplinary rehab to people whose lives had been changed catastrophically through injury or accident. It was agreed that it would be the right place for the next part of Seán's journey. At the NRH he'd be able to avail of skilled speech, occupational and physical therapy which would hopefully get him further down the road to recovery. However, he'd have to wait his turn. His name was put on the waiting list, but no one knew how long it might take for a place to become available. Potentially Seán was going to remain in Beaumont for some time. I asked his doctors at Beaumont could I arrange for extra physiotherapy for Seán. I was happy to pay someone to come in and spend some time on his very damaged left side and his right side which was gaining strength. I felt it would better prepare him for his stay at the NRH, whenever that might happen. Eventually I was told it wouldn't be possible because of insurance. But luck was on my side as my nephew, Peter's son Dylan, was training to be a physiotherapist. Every few days he'd arrive to visit Seán and behind the curtain he began to work his magic. He did exercises on Seán's shoulder and hip to loosen them up and increase the range of motion Seán had in that area. It was something at least. The signs were also there that Seán had become more aware of his surroundings but what if Seán was waiting months for a bed in the NRH? Could we manage as a family to keep him stimulated and engaged for a prolonged period? I wasn't sure.

I decided I was going to try again to improve the experience Seán was having. I requested a meeting of all the people who were involved with Seán's care: his consultant, nursing team, physiotherapists, speech and language and occupational therapists. The multidisciplinary team meeting was arranged for the following week and I asked Seán's family to come with me. The night before, I sat up in bed writing notes. I'd kept track of everything: significant dates and days over the previous weeks. I knew what I wanted to say. Seán's medical needs had been met but that was it. We had come across some incredibly kind and dedicated healthcare staff but, unfortunately, we had also met a lot of people who made life so much harder than it needed to be. I thought back on how upset I felt about Seán not being dressed, seeing him there exposed with no dignity in a busy hospital. I remembered the fear of walking into the ward to find Seán with so much fluid in his mouth I thought he was going to choke. I remembered how angry I was the day I discovered Seán had slept the whole way through his speech therapy, yet his file read that he had completed the session.

The meeting was held in a board room in the hospital. We entered and took our seats around a big table. About 20 faces looked back at me, faces I had become familiar with over the previous weeks. I began. Calmly and chronologically I outlined my concerns. When I finished, I looked up from my notes and asked, 'Would you be happy if this was your husband, your brother or your dad?' Everyone looked down. They couldn't answer me.

We Don't Do Miracles

Life went on and the summer months of 2018 passed us by. We continued to do as much as we could as a family to keep Seán engaged and stimulated until a place became available for him at the NRH in Dún Laoghaire. I still hadn't returned to work at Dunnes Stores since the attack so I spent my days with Seán, by his bedside in Beaumont Hospital, hoping the day would come soon. And then one day the call came. It was Seán's turn; he was finally going to get the intensive brain therapy he so badly needed. A woman rang my mobile to tell me the good news. I felt such relief that the time had come for Seán and us as a family to embark on the next part of our journey. Before the woman hung up from the call, she said to me, 'Martina, remember we don't do miracles in the NRH.' I had to catch my breath. I knew what she was trying to say but what a way to say it. I was aware of the severity of Seán's injuries, but I had to remain optimistic. The warning seemed cruel and insensitive to me. It wasn't the first time I had been taken aback by the way bad news was delivered. A few days beforehand Professor Mark Delargy, the Clinical Director at the NRH, had come to visit us in Beaumont. We went into a little side room with a nurse to chat through different elements of Seán's care. Suddenly I felt an impulse to ask a question I'd never asked before. It was an issue we had skirted around many times in different meetings, but I was always too afraid to ask it directly. For some reason the words came out. 'Will Seán walk again?' I asked Professor Delargy. Without missing a beat, he replied, 'No.' It felt like someone had stabbed me in the heart. It was a definitive no. Late that night I drove along the M50 on my way home. I was devastated. I remember thinking I needed wipers for my eyes because the tears just kept falling.

Professor Delargy's prediction was not a massive shock to me but nonetheless I felt winded by the news. I knew how profound Seán's brain injury was and that it meant his chances of ever walking again were slim. I had asked the question out straight; I should have been ready for the answer. But I couldn't help but feel hurt by the way it was delivered. The next day the nurse rang me on my mobile to see if I was okay. 'He should have waited to answer that question when you had some of the family with you,' she said. She was right. It wouldn't have made any difference to Seán's prognosis but at least I would have had some support in that moment. I didn't have time to dwell on any of this because we were on the move, finally. We prepared Seán for what was about to happen and on 3 September 2018 we arrived in Dún Laoghaire full of hope. Usually people are admitted to the NRH for a 12-week stay but that can change depending on the severity of a person's injuries. It was clear from the beginning that Seán would be there longer than that but we didn't know for how long exactly.

He was admitted to St Patrick's Ward where he joined around 10 other patients: men and women of all ages with a variety of different brain injuries. He was placed right under the nurses' station, which came as a massive relief to me. Seán still couldn't communicate so I was delighted to know if he had an issue with anything someone would notice. The building was old, but the staff were all professional and friendly. Seán settled very quickly and I was hopeful he was going to improve. He was finally in the right place to get the intensive brain rehab he needed, the physio, the speech and language, the occupational therapy, whatever help was on offer. While still at Beaumont he had been prescribed Ritalin, a drug sometimes given to people with ADHD to help improve their attention span. It can also be beneficial to some people with brain injuries and it worked for Seán. A new schedule was established for Seán involving occupational therapy, physiotherapy and speech and language therapy.

Seán was still being peg fed when he arrived at the NRH. This meant all his nutrients, fluid and medications were being put directly into his stomach via a feeding tube. He hadn't drunk or eaten anything normally since the attack, so one of the first medical goals was to address that. It was done in a very similar way to how babies are weaned onto solid food. It starts with a small spoonful of puréed food and then over time the quantity is increased. It must be done gradually and with great care, especially in Seán's case, as his swallow had been compromised from the weeks with the tracheostomy inserted. At first someone held the spoon for him but as Seán's strength increased, he started to do it himself. He took to it like a duck to water. He began to enjoy spoons of puréed sausage, mash and peas, chicken curry or pork – whatever was on the menu on a given day. A sippy cup was then introduced for liquids and as time went on Seán progressed to two and then three meals a day. Someone had to be with him in case a piece of food went down the wrong way but nonetheless it was so wonderful to see him do something we all take for granted every day: enjoying a meal. Snacks with more texture were then introduced, meaning his many visitors could bring him in a little treat, which he was delighted about. On a Sunday evening the staff came around with ice-cream for everyone. At the beginning Seán couldn't have one but eventually he got to the stage where he could accept the treat. He devoured those ice-creams. I guess you only realise how much you love something when you can't have it anymore.

At this stage I decided to return to work part time. After the attack my boss, Mrs Heffernan, had asked me to come to see her and her daughter Anne. We spent some time together in her office. We had tea. We were both upset. I told her how badly injured Seán was and how long the road ahead of us was. We also talked about my efforts to make sure Seán got the rehabilitation he needed and deserved. She knew I had a fight on my hands, and she knew how much it was going to cost. She made it very clear that day that the company would support me in any way they could and since then they have gone above and beyond expectations to do just that. Before I left her office that day she told me she admired my dedication and commitment to Seán and encouraged me to do whatever I had to do to continue to be his voice. As she headed out the door, she turned and said, 'Martina, I always knew you were tough.' At first it took me a minute to realise what she was talking about. 'I remember that range review years ago and the way you handled it,' she said. 'It just shows you, what doesn't kill you makes you stronger.' I knew she was right. I felt no pressure to go back but it had been almost six months since my last day in work, and I felt that I needed to regain some sense of normality. Life had been on hold, but now Seán's schedule of therapies meant I could work mornings and still spend the afternoons and evenings with him.

The days were long, but I got great comfort from being back in work. It felt like I was getting back a little bit of what life was like before the attack. It was great to be reunited with my friends and colleagues who had shown me such kindness and support; it gave me a real boost. Seán was in a good place. He was stable and comfortable and had settled into his new surroundings. He still had no words, though, as his speech centre had been badly damaged in the attack. But Seán didn't need words to make a friend. Paul Pilkington, who was in the same ward as Seán, had had a severe stroke. Very quickly they struck up a friendship, with Paul doing Seán's talking for him when he needed it. He was always looking out for Seán. He'd throw a ball to him and encourage him to throw it back to his bed. They watched *Mrs. Brown's Boys* together and Paul had an incredible ability to get Seán to laugh. On a Sunday, mass was held in the hospital and the two of them would go together. They used to sit side by side, both in their wheelchairs, holding hands. They were always up to mischief and it was incredible to watch the bond they developed. I became friendly with his wife, Valerie, who I still talk to regularly. We shared a grief for what our lives had been like before and a shared hope that our husbands would get better. Seán's friends from St Peter's GAA Club also became regular visitors to the NRH. They set up a rota and a WhatsApp group to keep everyone up to date on Seán's progress after each visit. 'Seán's Storytellers' did just that: they told Seán stories about sport and GAA and what was going on at the club. They were so good to him. Everyone was starting to notice an improvement in him: he was becoming more alert and engaged. It spurred us on to continue to do all we could to complement the professional help Seán was getting. He still had many tired days but there was no doubt he was beginning to take in more of what was going on around him. In a way I felt justified that I had pushed so hard to get Seán more rehab while he was still a patient in Beaumont. I had felt so many times that I was being difficult, but it never felt like I had a choice. One night as I sat on the side of his bed getting ready to say goodbye for the night, Emma asked him to point to the bossiest person in the room. Seán lifted his hand and pointed straight at me. Maybe he was right. But I was only doing what I knew he'd have done for me.

The Kindness of Friends and Strangers

rofessor Delargy's prediction that Seán wouldn't walk again had really floored me. It's not that I expected him to be walking and talking any time soon, but I was holding out hope that with intensive and prolonged rehab he would make some progress. I didn't talk to anyone outside the immediate family about the conversation. I don't really know why but I think somewhere in my head I thought if I told people it would be somehow set in stone. I always found it difficult to talk about Seán to people outside of our close circle – it felt like it was a betrayal of trust. If Seán could speak for himself would he reveal so much? I felt really alone. Then one day I met the chairman of St Peter's GAA Club, Fergus McNulty, who I had been in regular contact with since the attack. Seán trusted Fergus and I knew I could too. When Seán's time as chairman of the club was coming to an end he had asked Fergus to take over from him. Fergus wasn't convinced. He had a young family at the time and he knew how much work was involved. He also knew the role involved a lot of public speaking at meetings and different club events and he wasn't sure he wanted to take that on.

Over a pint Seán revealed to Fergus that he had found that part hard too. He opened up to Fergus that he never liked making speeches or being centre stage but he did it because he loved the club. He genuinely believed in the social good it can bring to a community and he was passionate about bringing people together, something he had done really successfully. By the time they left the pub, Fergus had been persuaded and they continued to work closely together at the club.

The McNulty family had run a nursing home, Marymount Care Centre, in Lucan for 30 years. Fergus made it clear that day that they were there to help Seán if he needed a nursing home at any stage over the course of his journey. I was still adamant that Seán was coming home eventually to our house, but I knew that at some point in between stints in rehab we may need some nursing home cover. It was a comfort to know that option was available to us if we needed it. During the conversation I confided in Fergus about what the consultant had told me. 'The doctors don't think Seán will ever walk again,' I said to him. 'We really do have such a long and uncertain road ahead of us.' I knew Fergus would respect Seán's privacy. I also admitted to Fergus that I felt alone. We were both really emotional. Fergus told me there was an army of people associated with St Peter's GAA Club who wanted to help. Seán was an integral part of the club, which had grown to more than 700 players. He had been club secretary and chairman and was currently the treasurer. He had overseen a lot of the club's development. Everyone knew him, everyone liked him and everyone wanted to help. Fergus explained that the club had been inundated with offers of support but he didn't want to do anything without my go-ahead. People were more than willing to play their part but they weren't sure what they should or could do. A number of senior people at the club had already had several conversations about possible fundraising initiatives but they were waiting for the green light from me.

Up to this point I'd given very little thought to fundraising for Seán. I was so caught up with just making sure he was getting through each day, I hadn't had much time to think long-term. A man called Emmet Kavanagh, from Tallaght in Dublin, had set up a GoFundMe page for Seán in the immediate aftermath of the attack. He had no connection to Seán personally but they had a shared passion: a love for Liverpool. Emmet had written, 'I've set this page up to help raise funds to cover Seán's medical expenses and expenses incurred by his family to help them stay by his side.' The page gained a lot of traction through shares on social media and people, many of them strangers, donated in their thousands. In the first eight hours of the page being live €15,000 had been raised. It was overwhelming really to think that someone would take it upon themselves to do this. Emmet was such a decent guy. Hearing that Seán would never walk again had really brought it home to me that the road ahead of us was going to be long and very costly. At this stage I was already beginning to wonder what would happen to Seán after his stint at the NRH came to an end, so I told Fergus I'd be happy for them to do whatever they thought they could do.

A few days later he called me and asked me to meet him in Dunboyne Castle Hotel for a coffee. It was there that I met Stephen Felle for the first time, a man I now speak to at least once a week. Stephen lives in Dunboyne and was also involved with St Peter's GAA Club. Stephen had been in Portugal with some friends on the day Seán was attacked. He had watched the Champions League Semi-final between Liverpool and Roma. The next morning, 25 April 2018, he headed for Faro airport to drop his friends off to get a flight back to Dublin. At the same time his wife and three children were flying from Dublin to Portugal for a holiday. As he waited in a coffee shop in the airport for their flight to arrive he checked his phone. He saw the news that a man from Meath who had travelled to Liverpool to watch the match had been attacked outside Anfield stadium and was badly injured. Then his phone rang. It was Fergus. 'There's been some bad news over here,' said Fergus. He went on to tell him that it was Seán Cox who had been attacked and that the prognosis wasn't good. Months later Fergus approached Stephen to see if he would be willing to get involved in St Peter's GAA Club's fundraising efforts. At the time Stephen was a senior executive at Davy Stockbrokers; he now owns a wealth management company called Argeau. Fergus knew that Stephen's corporate and financial background would be useful. Stephen agreed to do whatever he could do to help. Over coffee Fergus and Stephen explained to me that they wanted to establish a committee of people who would investigate different ways to support Seán. A week later I received an email from Stephen Felle. Things had moved quickly. The 'Support Seán' website was up and running, a logo had been designed and the wheels were already in motion for a number of different events.

The first of them, a fun run, was planned for the October bank holiday weekend. It was to take place in the village of Dunboyne. I felt really nervous about it. I knew people felt awful over what had happened to Seán and we had been shown such compassion. The community of Dunboyne had already thrown their arms around us as a family, but I felt awkward about asking people to come out for a big event like this. For the fundraising committee it was also a bit of a baptism by fire. They knew around a thousand people had subscribed to the race online. They were hoping another thousand might turn up on the day. The aim was to hopefully raise €10,000 for Seán. I remember Stephen Felle later telling me that on the morning of the run they realised they had no water for the runners so they had to borrow a van and make a last-minute dash to Musgrave's wholesaler to buy some. The run was to begin and end at St Peter's GAA Club. Myself and Jack, Shauna and Emma had been asked to start the race and had been given white T-shirts with 'Support Seán' written on them. Mine had '1' on it and the children had 2, 3 and 4. We headed off for the GAA club not really knowing what to expect. It was mild and dry and as I turned the corner into the car park all I could see was a sea of white T-shirts. 'Support Seán' in red writing was everywhere I looked. I couldn't believe it. It was so emotional knowing all these people were there for Seán.

The village was thronged. Local people had volunteered their time to cordon off the streets and make sure everyone was safe. Hardcore athletes from several running clubs had turned up along with lots of families with children in buggies. Seán's family was there, my family, our friends and my colleagues from Dunnes Stores. A huge crowd from Seán's work, Precision Cables in Dundalk, turned up to show their support too. After the run we all gathered in the clubhouse for soup and sandwiches. So many people came over to tell me that Seán had been in their thoughts and prayers and to offer their help in whatever way I needed it. Over 4,000 people showed up that day: all ages, all abilities, all there for Seán. Inside the bar of the clubhouse, which had been closed off, the committee members sat around counting the money that had been raised. There was €40,000 for the 'Support Seán' fund. They just couldn't believe it. They hadn't expected to raise so much money and now they didn't know where to put it. It was a weekend so the banks and the credit union were closed. The decision was made to put a call in with a local publican in the village to see if he had a safe. He obliged, so Stephen Felle put the money into a SuperValu bag and deposited it safely for the night. We were all truly blown away. For me, the turnout, the support and the good will really symbolised the contribution Seán had made to the community over the previous years. He was very much a part of Dunboyne life. Maybe it was true that you get back what you put in. The success of that first event really emboldened the fundraising committee to keep going. Seán's story had obviously hit a nerve with people. A husband and father doing something he loved to do when the unimaginable happened. They wanted to support him.

Several fundraisers followed. Around 4,000 people turned out on a cold and wet December evening to watch Meath take on Dublin in Pairc Tailteann in Navan. That was a particularly emotional occasion for me because of

Seán's intense love for the GAA and his close association with both Dublin and Meath. It was so wonderful seeing so many people come out to support Seán, but I couldn't help feeling so sad that Seán couldn't be there himself. As time went on, the decision was made to establish the 'Seán Cox Rehabilitation Trust'. People had shown us such generosity and I felt it was important to make sure there was proper governance around the money that was raised. Stephen Felle agreed. The fundraising committee tried to establish the potential cost of Seán's care into the future. It was a difficult task because there were still so many unknowns, but we did know that Seán had a normal life expectancy and he would need rehab for the rest of his life. We also knew it was going to have to be funded privately and it was going to run into millions of euro. The committee set itself a target to raise €2 million. It was an ambitious aim, and I wanted to make sure it was done properly. It was vital that everything was above board from a revenue and tax point of view but also reputationally. Stephen sought legal advice and our fundraising efforts were formalised. The Seán Cox Rehabilitation Trust was established with an independent board of trustees and Stephen Felle as chairman. If people were going to be kind enough to donate their hard-earned cash to help Seán get the help he badly needed, I wanted them to know that was exactly where their money was going.

People really had been so kind. In the aftermath of the attack I heard from people right around the world. Liverpool FC supporters from every corner of Ireland and the UK had written to me. But it didn't stop there. I also heard from many people who weren't Reds fans. A man I don't know, Michael from Dublin, wrote to me to tell me he was praying for Seán. 'As a Man United fan,' he said, 'I can't believe I'm saying this, but I hope Liverpool win the Champions League and you are able to see it.' Everyone was horrified that Seán had been so badly injured in such a vicious attack. I was offered prayers and holy medals, poems and positive thoughts and everything in between. When Seán had still been in The Walton Centre in Liverpool we had been inundated with offers of help, many of them from Irish people living in Liverpool. One of them, Gráinne, who was originally from Dublin, wrote to me saying, 'Myself and my husband are Kop season ticket holders, and we are both deeply saddened by the tragic, barbaric and unnecessary events that have occurred, we want to offer our support in any way we can, we live close to the airport and if you need any help from a fellow Irish Red please do not hesitate to contact us.' Lifts, accommodation, food, a shoulder to cry on. Nothing was too much for the people who were offering us their support.

I also heard from people I hadn't been in touch with for years. One day I got a letter from a girl I had gone to school with, Jackie Mullins. She lived on the road beside us and we had walked to school together many times. In her letter she urged me to fight to get Seán as much rehab as possible. We arranged to meet up a few months later. 'Did you ever receive an anonymous donation to the Seán Cox Trust?' Jackie asked me over coffee. 'I'm not sure,' I replied. Most of the donations were generally accompanied by a message of support from the person or organisation making the donation. 'But a big one,' she said, 'like a large sum?' I remembered Stephen Felle telling me there had been some substantial donations that had taken the trustees by surprise. 'Why?' I asked her, intrigued. She went on to tell me she had donated to the fund herself, but she wanted to do more. She'd racked her brains to think of someone with money. 'The nuns have lots of it,' she said. So she traced the Sisters of St Paul the Apostle back to Birmingham in England and got in contact with them. She explained that the husband of a past pupil has been attacked and left with a serious brain injury and needed a lot of rehabilitation. She asked them to consider donating to the Seán Cox Rehabilitation Trust. They wrote back to her and told her that they would, but it would have to be an anonymous donation. I couldn't believe it. A girl I hadn't seen in more than 30 years, an old friend, had done that for Seán. I was completely blown away by how smart Jackie Mullins is. And how kind she is too. Another day I opened a letter from a six-year-old boy named Isaac from Maynooth in Co. Kildare. He explained he was a fellow Liverpool fan and that he hoped Seán would get better soon. He had enclosed a €5 note, stuck to the inside of the card, which he said was 'to buy stuff'. Men, women and children, people of all ages, from close to home and further away, some part of the Liverpool family and some not, were behind us. In the darkest of moments, of which there were many, I always knew we weren't walking this road alone.

The Most Important of the Least Important Things

S even months after Seán was attacked, I found myself with Jack on a plane to Liverpool. I was going to meet the then CEO of Liverpool FC, Peter Moore. In the very early days after Seán was attacked, I had received a letter from the Liverpool manager, Jürgen Klopp. He explained he wanted to reach out to let us know that Seán was in his and the club's thoughts and prayers. He went on to write that 'in a few days Liverpool could become champions of Europe. It would be a magnificent achievement and one that everyone at the club and everyone who supports us would regard as something truly momentous. And yet at the same time I would trade any of the glory that could come our way for Seán to get back to his full health and to be back at home with you and all of his loved ones'. He said that although football is a major part of his life, he knows that it is the most important of the least important things. 'Health, happiness and family are what matters most and there are no trophies in the world that matter more than those things.' The letter was genuine and heartfelt. In the final paragraph he wrote, 'Putting my football manager's hat on for a moment, it is important for me to know that we, as a club, are supporting Seán and his family just as he has always supported us. So, if you feel there is anything we can do to help please let us know.' The letter was signed, 'You'll Never Walk Alone, Jürgen Klopp'. I couldn't help but wonder what Seán's reaction would be to me getting a personal letter from one of his all-time sporting heroes. It would have been funny if it wasn't so tragic.

Jack and I landed in Liverpool early on the morning of 12 November 2018 and made our way to Liverpool's corporate offices on Chapel Street in the city. I knew Peter Moore was a die-hard Reds fan. He was originally from the city but had worked in America for years before returning to take up the position of CEO of Liverpool FC in 2017, a position he would hold until retiring in August 2020. We had engaged a solicitor in the UK, so Stephen Jones from the law firm Leigh Day was also attending the meeting. I knew at this stage that Seán was going to need care for the rest of his life. I also knew that any recovery gains he would make over the coming months and years would very much depend on how much rehab he received. This was going to have to be privately funded and it wasn't going to come cheap. The local people in Dunboyne had shown us such enormous generosity in helping us to fundraise for Seán's care. People right around the country who didn't know us had also donated while Liverpool fans in Ireland and the UK had come out in their thousands to support Seán. A.S. Roma football club had also contacted me in the days after Seán was attacked. I received a letter from the club's CEO, Umberto Gandini, who said he was 'writing with a heavy heart knowing how difficult and devastating this time is for you and your family'. He went on to say that everyone at the club was absolutely horrified and sickened by the scenes outside Anfield, and they were truly sorry for what had happened and the grief and heartache that had been caused to us. 'These people are not football fans and don't represent A.S. Roma, these people are criminals and the perpetrators of this grotesque attack must be brought to justice,' said Gandini. He also assured me that the club had been helping all of the authorities with their investigations – the Merseyside Police, the Italian Special Police, UEFA and Liverpool FC in the hope that those responsible would be punished accordingly. He finished his letter by saying that no one should ever end up in hospital after travelling to attend a football match. 'This is not football; this is not the sport we all love.' A.S. Roma FC wanted to send a representative to the hospital to see me and to say sorry in person, but I was too consumed with everything that was going on with Seán at the time to even give it a second thought. Months later I told Fergus McNulty and Stephen Felle about the letter and they contacted the club. A.S. Roma's general manager and head of marketing later came to Dublin to meet with us. They were genuinely horrified at what had happened and donated €150,000 to Seán's rehab.

Liverpool FC had stayed in contact with me since the attack, and I'd spoken to the club's liaison officer, Tony Barrett, several times. He had also stayed in close contact with Marty since Seán had been transferred from The Walton Centre to Beaumont Hospital. Liverpool FC had been so helpful in those early days, organising and paying for flights and accommodation so our family could visit

Seán. I had felt very supported by the people at the club, the players and the fans from the get-go. But the reality of the situation was that Seán would never work again, and the cost of his care was going to run into millions of euro. As we arrived to meet Peter Moore, I hoped the club, which Seán had supported since he was a boy, might be able to help. We were welcomed into his office and introduced to Peter. He was very sympathetic about what had happened and genuinely interested in how Seán was doing. I filled him in on how Seán had gotten on at Beaumont and the progress he was making at the NRH. I felt very emotional during the meeting. It was strange to find myself in that situation – one I'd never have been in if what happened hadn't happened. Peter Moore assured us that Liverpool would not forget about Seán and that the club would do whatever it could to support us. I'm not quite sure what I was expecting from the meeting. The savage and brutal attack happened just metres from the stadium, but *not* on club property and *legally* the club didn't have a case to answer. But our lives had been turned upside-down and I needed Peter to hear that.

A few months later I was invited to meet Peter Moore in Liverpool again, but I was really preoccupied with Seán's care. I asked the chairman of the Seán Cox Rehabilitation Trust, Stephen Felle, to attend for me, and he agreed. The meeting was held on 4 January 2019, also in the club's corporate offices. Peter and Stephen hit it off and the meeting ended on a much more positive note. Liverpool FC's position hadn't changed – there was no recourse to the club for what had happened to Seán – however, they were serious about helping us in whatever way they could. Stephen stressed to

Peter that Seán was now lying in a hospital bed in Dublin. He would never be the same again and he would need care for the rest of his life. I think by the time the meeting came to an end the two men had found common ground. Stephen's corporate background meant he appreciated the fact that legally Liverpool FC had no case to answer. Peter gained a greater understanding of the personal loss we were feeling as a family and how our motivation was driven solely by a desire to do whatever we could to get as much of the old Seán back as possible. The Seán who travelled to watch his beloved team, like he had done hundreds of times before, didn't come home the same man. Peter Moore knew we needed help if we were going to be able to get Seán the care he needed. He then made a commitment that the club would throw its weight behind fundraising for Seán.

The seeds were sown for a Liverpool Vs Ireland Legends charity match in Dublin. Alongside this, Liverpool FC and its players were making a donation to Seán's care. We'd been shown a huge amount of love and support from the people of Liverpool city and fans of the club. They had really wrapped their arms around us. The supporters' group, Spirit of Shankly, had organised a bucket collection at Liverpool's home game against Cardiff City. It turned out to be one of the biggest ever bucket collections at Anfield. I was later told the volunteers on the day didn't even have to shake the buckets. People came to them to donate what they could. The club's official charity, Liverpool FC Foundation, matched the amount donated by fans on the day and €64,000 was raised. So many people from Liverpool had gotten in touch with me when Seán had been in The Walton Centre, many of whom had Irish roots. In letters, emails and cards they told me of their anger that one of their own, an Irish man and a Reds fan, had been left for dead in their city. The day after Seán was attacked Marty had to travel back to their hotel to collect their bags and their passports. When he got into the taxi, he gave the driver the address but asked him not to take the route that would bring them past Anfield. He hadn't slept in more than 24 hours and he was still in shock. He knew he couldn't be confronted with the scene of the crime. 'Are you related to that Irish guy who was attacked last night?' asked the taxi driver. 'He's my brother,' replied Marty. When he reached the hotel, the driver wouldn't allow him to pay the fare.

When Stephen returned from his meeting with Peter Moore with news of the club's commitment to help us, I'm not sure I believed it. As a child Peter Moore had stood in the same spot outside Anfield as Seán had when the attack happened. Armed with a pork pie and a cup of Bovril he'd waited with his dad, nervous and excited to see his team play. He'd spent more than 50 years loving and supporting Liverpool, the club he truly believed was the best in the world. I'd seen the words 'We are Liverpool, We are Family' emblazoned on flags and flashing on pitch-side hoardings at matches. Was it a clever marketing slogan? Or was it more than that? Only time would tell.

Fairy Lights and Laughter

Our first Christmas since Seán had been attacked was approaching. I was dreading it and wasn't sure how we'd get through it. It was our favourite time of the year and for us, like so many other Irish families, it was all about family and tradition. Every year we did the exact same thing. On Christmas Eve Seán would take Jack, Shauna and Emma to his cousin Richard's house for mince pies. I'd stay at home to get the house organised. They'd come back to collect me, and we'd all go to Christmas Eve mass together in St Peter and Paul's church in the village. Afterwards we'd head to our local Italian restaurant, La Bucca, for a family meal. The five of us would sit and chat over pizza and pasta, excited about the days ahead. When we got home, we'd sit down to a Christmas movie. Even as the children turned into teenagers, they never ventured out on Christmas Eve. They were happy to spend that evening with us and we always kept the same tradition. Santa also continued to visit our house well into the teenage years, but not until everyone was in bed. Once they headed up me and Seán made sure everything was organised. The next morning

Sineád's Communion in May 1986 with Seán's mam and dad, and his siblings Peter, Martin and Suzanne.

Outside the Kilternan Hotel where family and friends gathered for our wedding day on 8 July 1989. We had only been together a year when Seán proposed.

At a friend's wedding in late 1989. We had only been married a few months ourselves. I picked out Seán's suit for the occasion!

On holidays in Spain in 2003. Emma was just two, Shauna four and a half, and Jack six – all full of energy and great fun to be around.

July 2011 on a trip to Slide 'n' Splash while on holiday in Portugal. This became an annual trip, something the kids so looked forward to. It wasn't Seán's favourite place because of his fear of water, but that didn't matter because the kids loved it.

Family holiday in Lagos, Portugal, in 2016. The kids at this point were going on holidays with their friends but never turned down the opportunity for us all to be together in Lagos.

Lagos in July 2017. Our special place. Little did I know this would be the last photo of us together here or what lay ahead for us in 2018.

Galway 2012. Seán at his niece Aisling's 21st birthday with Martin, Sineád, Suzanne and Peter. Family gatherings were always important to Seán, especially as both his parents had passed away, so it was always good to be together.

Seán and Richard after a night run. This is very special as it is the last photo taken of Seán just two days before the attack. To see him so fit and full of enthusiasm takes my breath away.

Shauna and I outside Preston Crown Court speaking to the media after Simone Mastrelli was jailed for three and a half years for the assault on Seán. (© *Richard McCarthy/PA Archive/PA Images*)

Emma, myself, Shauna and Jack at the start line of a Family Fun Run in Dunboyne in October 2018, the first fundraiser organised for Seán. Great community spirit that day; we were totally blown away by the turn out for the event.

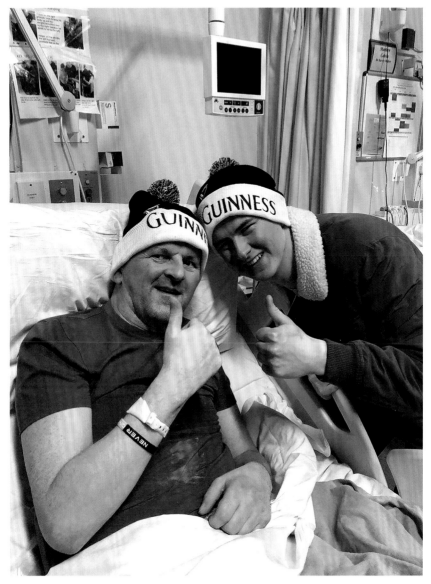

Jack with his dad on Christmas Eve 2018 in the National Rehabilitation Hospital. Jack decided to get into the Christmas Spirit and they both wore matching Guinness hats.

Liverpool players Gini Wijnaldum and Andy Robertson holding up Seán's banner after Liverpool beat Napoli 5-0 at the Aviva Stadium. (© *Action Plus Sports/ Alamy Live News*)

Saen Cox
I hope you are ok.
I iknow you support.
Liverpool i support Liverpool.
too and here's 5Euro to Buy.
Stuff. From Isaac.

A lovely note and a donation for Seán from a very thoughtful little boy: a small example of the huge support we have received from friends and strangers alike over the last few years.

3rd May 2018

Dear Martina

I was greatly saddened and appalled to hear of the terrible attack on your husband Seán in Liverpool.

The outpouring of solidarity to you, Jack, Shauna, Emma and Seán comes, not only from the soccer community of which he is a part, but from all of us who love and support sport.

The many tributes that have been paid to Seán during the past week speak of a man who is held in the highest regard and affection within the community. I wish to assure you and your family of my solidarity at this difficult and distressing time.

Be assured that Sabina and I will keep Seán in our thoughts and prayers.

Beir beannacht

Yours sincerely

Michael D. Higgins
Úachtarán na hÉireann
President of Ireland

This very thoughtful letter from President Michael D. Higgins arrived in Dunboyne when Seán was in a coma in the Walton Centre in Liverpool.

**Liverpool Football Club
& Athletic Grounds Limited
Melwood Training Ground**
Melwood Training Ground, Deysbrook Lane,
West Derby, Liverpool, L12 8SY
Tel: +44 (0)151 282 8888 Fax: +44 (0)151 252 2206
www.liverpoolfc.com

Dear Mrs Cox,

I hope you do not mind me contacting you by letter. I know you have requested privacy for the time being and of course we have respected that but I thought it was important that I reach out to you to let you know that Sean and all of his family remain in our thoughts and prayers.

In a few days, Liverpool could become champions of Europe. It would be a magnificent achievement and one that everyone at the club and everyone who supports us would regard as something truly momentous. And yet at the same time I would trade any of the glory that could come our way for Sean to get back to full health and to be back at home with you and all of his loved ones.

Although football has always been a major part of my life, I have also known that it is the most important of the least important things. Health, happiness and family are what matters most and there are no trophies in the world that matter more than any of those things. That is why I say that the biggest prize for everyone associated with Liverpool right now would be to know that Sean is going to return to full health as soon as possible.

I am reliably informed that you are not a football fan so that is why I am sending you this letter in the spirit of one parent to another. I have also been told that you have a loving family around you and having met your son, Jack, I get the impression that your children care for their mum and dad so much that I have no doubt that Sean could ask no more from those around him.

Putting my football manager's hat on for moment, it is important to me to know that we, as a club, are supporting Sean and his family just as he has always supported us. So if you feel that there is anything that we can do to help please let us know. I understand that Tony Barrett has been in regular contact so please continue to speak to him so that we will know when the time is right for Sean to receive visitors and also to allow us to understand what we can do for you.

It goes without saying that there is no need for you to reply to this letter. I just wanted to let you know that Sean and yourselves are in as thoughts as much as ever. As a person of faith I will continue to pray for you all and hopefully the prayers of myself and countless other people will soon be answered.

You'll Never Walk Alone

Jürgen Klopp

We had just got Seán back to Beaumont Hospital when this lovely letter arrived from Liverpool FC Manager Jürgen Klopp.

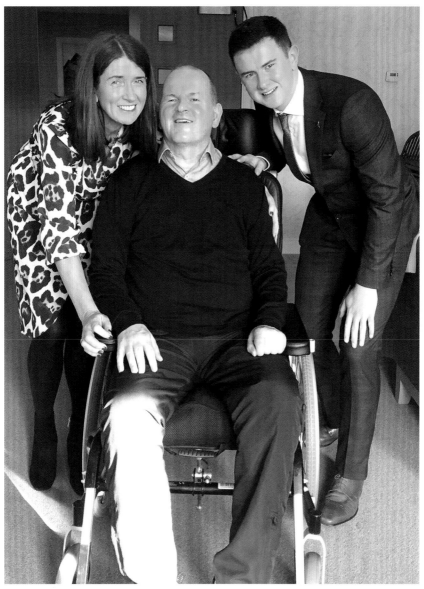

November 2019. Myself, Seán and Jack heading to Anfield for the first time since the attack. An emotional day.

April 2019 at a fundraiser for Seán in the Aviva Stadium: Liverpool legends take on the Ireland legends. Seán was starstruck in the company of Mick McCarthy, Ian Rush, Kenny Dalglish and Peter Moore.

Seán meets Jürgen Klopp for the first time. Both were very happy to meet each other.

Seán meets Ian Rush in Anfield in November 2019.

Seán with Martin, Peter and Suzanne. This was Seán and Martin's first time in Anfield together since the attack.

September 2019. The family all gathering to say their goodbyes as Seán leaves Marymount Care Centre to start a rehabilitation programme in STEPS, Sheffield. As a family we were a bit apprehensive about the next stage of Seán's journey, but the 14-week stint in STEPS was such a positive experience for Seán and had a big impact on his rehabilitation.

A comedy fundraiser for Seán in January 2020 organised by John Bishop. An amazing night. The roof lifted when the crowd sang 'You'll Never Walk Alone' at the end of the night.

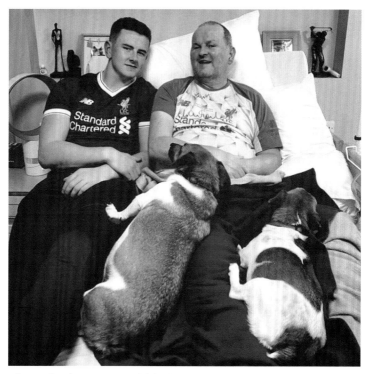

The night that Liverpool lifted the Premier League Cup. Jack and Seán, with his guard dogs Bruno and Roxy forever at his side.

March 2020. The day we had been waiting for for so long had finally arrived. Just two years, two hospitals, two rehab facilities and a nursing home later, Seán finally made it home where he belongs.

there was one rule; we all had to go downstairs together. The magic was well and truly alive in our house.

In 2013 my mam, Ann, had passed away. She was diagnosed with lymphoma in January of that year and died in February. She was in her late seventies but had been relatively healthy until then. My dad and my brother Terence lived together so they always came to our house for their dinner on Christmas Day. But this year was going to be very different. As the time got closer, I started to dread it more and more. I just couldn't bring myself to stay at home – it would be unbearable without Seán. I couldn't do what we had always done with Seán without him. It just wasn't possible. I also felt so sorry for my poor dad, who was 85 at this stage. He had taken the attack on Seán very badly. They had always had a very close and, in some ways, unique relationship. My dad loved horse racing and one of his favourite things to do over the years was go to the Listowel Races in Co. Kerry. When my mam passed away my dad stopped going. I think he lost confidence in himself to drive the distance from Dublin to The Kingdom. Seán knew my Dad missed it, so he offered to bring him. Off they went for a few days, taking in the horse racing and the Kerry scenery. My dad is a creature of habit, so they always did the exact same thing each time they went. Seán would bring him to the famous John B. Keane's pub for a pint even though my dad had never had a drink in his life. And they always went for a seaweed bath, of all things. The pair of them had a ball, comfortable in each other's company. Seán didn't have to offer to do that for my dad, but he wanted to. That was the way he was. He was very aware of what was going on in other people's lives and if he could help at all he would. My dad adored Seán. After the attack it took him a while to bring himself to go to visit him. I think it really hurt him to see his son-in-law so badly injured.

Christmas 2018 was going to be very different for me, Jack, Shauna and Emma but it was also going to be different for my dad. We were all feeling the loss. The whole family was hurting. We knew Seán wasn't well enough to leave the NRH even for a few hours, so there was only one option left. We'd go to him. I remember getting dressed up and arriving over to him on Christmas morning. It all felt so strange. I had organised presents for Jack, Shauna and Emma. I put them in envelopes and gave them to Seán to hand out. As each one of them opened their envelope they started to cry. Then I started to cry. As we sat there with tears rolling down our faces, Seán started to laugh. I think he thought we were all mad. My sister Catherine had offered to have us for dinner, so we travelled to her house for something to eat to allow Seán to rest and then we went back to him for the afternoon. We pretty much spent the day in the car. Over the years I'd often thought about how hard it must be for people to be in hospital at Christmas time and for their families not to have them at home. I'd often seen snippets on the news of doctors and nurses doing their best for their patients or photographs in the newspapers of Santa bringing some much-needed joy to sick children who couldn't go home for Christmas. I think I fooled myself into imagining it would be all singing and laughter. But it wasn't. It was bleak. The staff at the NRH did their best to make the day special for their patients but I felt desperately sad and lonely for the Christmases that had gone before. Our lives had been turned upside-down and no amount of fairy lights could take away the darkness. As we drove home along the M50 that night I remember Shauna saying, 'It could be worse, it could be our first Christmas without Dad.' It stopped me in my tracks. A much-needed dose of perspective.

As the new year dawned, I had to start thinking about what was next for Seán. The NRH is Ireland's only rehabilitation hospital. What would happen to Seán when his stay there was over? We had to be ready for our next move, whenever that came. I met regularly with the people who were caring for Seán in Dún Laoghaire. In one of those meetings Professor Delargy mentioned The Royal Hospital Donnybrook in Dublin as an option. He described it as a 'step-down facility' and said Seán wouldn't get as much rehabilitation there as he was receiving in the NRH, but it was an option. He also advised us to investigate rehab options in Germany and mentioned a man called Pádraig Schaler. Pádraig, who is from Glasnevin in Dublin, had suffered a serious brain injury after he was knocked off his bike in Cape Cod while in the US on his J1 trip in 2013. The 23-year-old had just finished his studies at Trinity College, Dublin. Like Seán, Pádraig had almost died but was saved after undergoing emergency surgery at a Cape Cod Hospital before being transferred back to Dublin. Myself, Sinéad and Richard arranged a meeting with Pádraig's parents, Reinhard Schaler and Patricia O'Byrne. They explained to us that when they brought their son back from the US to Dublin, there was literally nowhere for him to go. They were adamant that Pádraig wasn't going to end up in a nursing home. He was facing months in an acute hospital while he waited for a place at the NRH, which could take up to a year. Reinhard and Patricia had written a letter to the then Taoiseach Enda Kenny in 2014 titled 'The Broken Health System' in which they spoke about 'Ireland's appalling lack of adequate neuro-rehabilitation care which had been described as unethical and grotesque by experts in the field'. They said Ireland had failed their son and 'forced him from the country he loves more than any other'. Relocating to Germany for Pádraig's treatment was their only option. When there, Pádraig had gone on to improve in ways no one ever thought he would. But there was one catch.

Treatment in Germany was only possible for Pádraig because his father was a German citizen. This was not an option for Seán. I was beginning to realise that Seán's journey was going to be even more complicated than I had originally thought. Thousands of people suffer brain injuries in Ireland every year as a result of road crashes, strokes, falls and tumours. And then there were those, like Seán, who had been assaulted. I knew all of these people needed unique treatment to empower them to reach their full potential in terms of recovery. But where did these people end up? Were some of them in acute hospitals without access to adequate rehab? Were they living indefinitely in nursing homes long before their time? I knew there was no clear pathway for people like Seán, but it also seemed there was no support either. We were on our own for the next leg of this journey. But first I had to deal with something I had been dreading even more than Christmas.

Preston Crown Court

'I want to deliver the victim impact statement,' said Shauna. My instinct was to say no. She was only 20 years old and I felt it would be too much for her to have to go through, but she was adamant she wanted to do it. Three Roma supporters had been charged in connection with the chaos outside Anfield on 24 April 2018. Six months earlier, 29-year-old Daniele Suisco from Rome was the first man to appear in court. He was jailed for two and a half years for his part in the violent disorder on the evening Seán was attacked. It had been a straightforward sentence hearing because he pleaded guilty, so we hadn't travelled to the UK for it. At the sentencing, Judge Mark Brown said there was no doubt in his mind that the group of 'ultras' were intent on violence on the day in question. Now we were preparing for the trial of the third and final man, Simone Mastrelli, at which we'd also be given an opportunity to deliver a victim impact statement. There was so much going on with Seán, making sure he was getting the care he needed and making decisions for the future, it was hard to find the head space for the court cases too. Nevertheless, it had to be done.

Four months earlier, we had attended the trial of the second man involved, 21-year-old Filippo Lombardi. 'You're not going,' Jack had said to me repeatedly in the run up to it. 'It'll be too much for you, Mam, let me go.' He tried so hard to convince me to stay at home. But I wouldn't hear of it. I had to go. I knew if the shoe was on the other foot Seán would have gone for me. It was non-negotiable. Lombardi's trial was scheduled to take place over several days in October 2018. The case was to be heard in Preston Crown Court. We agreed that myself and Jack would attend, accompanied by Marty and his wife, Ruth, Peter and his wife, Aisling, and Seán's sister, Suzanne. Seán's other sister, Sinéad, agreed to stay in Ireland and take care of Seán who wasn't long in the NRH in Dún Laoghaire at that stage. I wanted someone familiar to be able to visit him while we were away. Lisa Hurst, our liaison officer from the Metropolitan Police in Liverpool, who I had met on that first day when I had arrived at The Walton Centre, prepped me as best she could for the trial. They didn't know how long it might go on for and they really had no idea what way it might go. Lombardi pleaded guilty to violent disorder at an earlier hearing. He was now facing a charge of grievous bodily harm to Seán, which he denied.

We arrived in Preston, which is one of the most depressing places I've ever been. We booked ourselves into a Premier Inn hotel which was right opposite the courthouse. When I checked into my room, I could see the entrance to the court from my window. 'What lies behind those doors?' I wondered to myself. I had never been inside a courtroom before in all my life. My only reference points were taken from trials I'd seen on TV and in movies. 'I swear by Almighty God that the evidence I shall give shall be the truth, the whole truth, and nothing but the truth.' Is that how it worked? I'd soon know. My first time in a courtroom was going to be for the trial of a man accused of inflicting grievous bodily harm on my husband. My perfectly fit and healthy husband, who was now severely brain damaged and unable to walk or talk. Lisa Hurst also warned me that the courtroom itself was very small and that we would inevitably be sitting very close to Lombardi's family. She also explained that Lombardi would be brought through from the back and would be sitting behind a glass panel. She told me I'd only see him if I looked around, and that I didn't have to do that. If I wanted to avoid seeing his face I could.

The next morning, we walked across to the courthouse to take our places. I felt sick with nerves. We were shown to the gallery, which was on the right-hand side of the courtroom. We took our seats, filling up the front row. Within minutes Lombardi's family entered the room. His mother and his sisters sat in the row right behind us. I just froze, I couldn't look around, so I just stared right ahead of me. The jury box was to our left and the judge was to the far right. Then Lombardi was brought in. It's very difficult to describe the feeling in the room. It was tense, you could almost smell the fear. I kept telling myself not to look around, to stare straight ahead and stay focused. But I couldn't. I had to see the whites of his eyes. I had to know what this man looked like. I turned my head and there he was. One of the men who had ripped our lives apart. The minute I saw him, I felt a familiar feeling deep in my stomach. It was the same feeling I had the very first time I laid eyes on Seán in the intensive care unit of The Walton Centre, lying there so badly injured and helpless. Now I felt it again bubbling inside me. It was rage.

As I turned my head back around to face the front of the court, I took a deep breath and exhaled slowly. Deep down I knew I had to let that feeling go. Instinctively I knew that if I let the anger get in on me, I would end up down a road I didn't want to be on. My priority now was Seán. It was my job to be his voice, to advocate for him, to make sure I did whatever I could to get him as much help as possible. Most importantly, I wanted to hold Seán's hand and guide him back to us. I couldn't do that if I let the anger eat away at me. Judge Mark Brown arrived to open the case. He started by outlining the injuries inflicted on Seán and how he was doing now. He was excellent and explained the process clearly, which I was relieved about as I had never had an experience like this before. The jury was then sworn in: six men and six women. The court service had arranged for us to have a family room in the courthouse which we used for breaks and lunch, so we didn't have to sit outside with Lombardi's family. Marty, who had witnessed the attack, was called to the stand to give his evidence. This was completely out of his comfort zone and he was understandably terribly nervous and emotional. He had been through such an ordeal and now here he was months later having to recount it step by step.

He told the court how delighted himself and Seán were when they had managed to secure the tickets in the days before the game. It was heartbreaking to watch him recall the events of that day. He described how he had met Seán at

Dublin Airport for their early morning flight on Tuesday 24 April 2018, excited about the day ahead. They had arrived safely in Liverpool city by half-past eight that morning. After having breakfast and a chat over a cup of tea, they had dropped their bags off at their hotel before taking a walk around the city. They had lunch and then made their way back to the hotel to check in. They showered before charging their phones and pulling on their jerseys. They had arranged to meet the man who had their tickets outside The Twelfth Man pub that evening. They jumped in a taxi and made their way to the grounds. The jury looked on as Marty explained that they had been expecting an electric atmosphere outside the stadium, but the buzz was better than they had ever imagined. As they made their way up Walton Breck Road, they heard noise: 'not good noises'. Within minutes they were surrounded by a group of up to 60 people wearing dark clothes, some of them with their faces covered. Marty turned to signal to Seán that it was time to get out of there when he realised he was lying on the ground. 'Seán, Seán, will ya wake up, come on,' he urged his older brother. Marty explained how he stayed gathered around him in fear that another attack was coming. He took a kick in the back which made him stumble but he steadied himself. Within a few seconds he felt the charge going past. They were gone. He told the court how a police officer and a steward arrived on the scene. Several Liverpool fans on their way into the ground also stopped to see if they could help. Marty kept looking at Seán, expecting him to move at any minute, to open his eyes. 'What's wrong with you? Come on Seán!' he urged again. The police officer moved Marty to the side so the steward could tend to Seán. 'That's my brother, that's my brother!' Marty had cried.

After what felt like an eternity to Marty, an ambulance arrived at the scene to bring Seán to Aintree University Hospital. Marty travelled in the back of the ambulance with him. He told how when they arrived at the hospital, he fully expected Seán to be bandaged up and discharged in an hour. 'I expected to be cursing him because we missed the game,' he said. Listening to Marty made me think again of the unfairness of it all. It was so hard to process that our life, which we had been so content with, had been so abruptly and drastically disrupted. In the blink of an eye everything had changed. And it only took seconds. Seventeen of them to be precise. Listening to Marty's evidence and that of the other witnesses was the hardest part of the trial for me. Harder than coming face to face with Lombardi. It wasn't so much the words they were speaking; it was their demeanour.

Everyone who was on Walton Breck Road that day and who had been caught up in what went on had been deeply traumatised by what had happened. One girl told how herself and her boyfriend were on their way to the match on the day in question when they saw a group of balaclava-clad men approaching. They had been near The Albert Pub on Walton Breck Road when they heard the chanting. Some of the men were waving their belts in the air. Her evidence was chilling. The case very much relied on the hours and hours of CCTV footage that the police had gathered from the area after the attack. Before any of it was shown, the judge gave a warning and I left the room each time. I didn't have it in me to watch it, and I never will. It was bad enough seeing the state Seán had been left in after the attack, I certainly didn't want to see the moment it had happened. I was just about keeping myself together and that would have been a step too far. Another witness contacted me after the trial was over. He was a young man from Liverpool who had also been there on the day. After witnessing the attack, he had sat with Marty as they waited for the ambulance to arrive for Seán. He had also captured the attack on his mobile phone, which he had surrendered to police. He contacted me to tell me how sorry he was about what had happened to Seán and to say if I was ever in Liverpool to get in touch with him. More than two years later he still sends me text messages to inquire about how Seán is doing.

Lombardi's legal team talked about his previous good character, how he was 'responsible and hardworking' and how he had played as goalkeeper in the A.S. Roma academy when he was a teenager. We didn't know when the trial would conclude. By Friday of that week we decided to go home for the weekend and return the following week. By Tuesday the jury was ready to return its verdict. We made our way across to the courtroom from the Premier Inn one last time, not knowing how this was going to go, trying not to second-guess the jury. A short time later they filed into the courtroom to deliver their verdict. I held my breath. Not guilty. A majority verdict. He was cleared of the charge of causing grievous bodily harm to Seán. Judge Mark Brown told Lombardi, 'There is no doubt in my mind that your purpose was to cause a violent clash with Liverpool fans, demonstrated vividly in film footage.' He said the CCTV had shown Lombardi had an active role in what happened that day as he was shown to use his belt 'like a whip'. He went on to say that football had been described as a beautiful game but the terrible events that took place that day in April 2018 have blighted its reputation.

Football's reputation was the last thing on my mind. I was devastated. Lombardi was handed a three-year sentence for the charge of violent disorder. The sentence didn't fit the crime. I couldn't get my head around it. Seán had been so severely injured that his life, our lives, would never be the same again. Seán was only at the very beginning of what we knew was going to be a very long road to recovery. Lombardi was going to prison for three years, at the very most, and could then resume his life as if nothing had happened at all. I had to get out of there. We left the court and crossed over the road to our hotel. The past week had been an emotional rollercoaster and now it had shuddered to a halt, but we felt Seán didn't get the justice he deserved. We sat around in the hotel lobby and decided to order a coffee and some lunch. Marty was particularly floored. In his eyes all three men should have been locked up for life, the keys thrown away. He felt Seán had been given a life sentence that day. Himself and Peter went outside to make some phone calls. Then suddenly we heard a commotion at the bar. A man had walked in off the street and was holding a staff member at knife point demanding money. I froze in my seat. Jack, who was beside me, went to jump up and help the girl, but I pulled him back. 'Sit down,' I said to him. In that moment all I could feel was sheer terror that something would also happen to Jack. Before we knew it two men who had been in the lobby managed to apprehend the man with the knife and put his arms behind his back as the police were called. We just grabbed our stuff and got out of there. I couldn't believe after the day we'd had we found ourselves in the middle of a hold-up. I thought to myself, 'If I don't laugh, I will cry.' So, I held on to Jack and we laughed. I swore I'd never return to Preston, but four months later we were preparing to return for the final time.

Packing a Punch

Thirty-year-old Simone Mastrelli had been extradited from Italy to the UK after being arrested on a European Arrest Warrant. He pleaded guilty to unlawfully and maliciously inflicting grievous bodily harm on Seán. He pleaded not guilty to a separate count of violent disorder, which had been accepted by the prosecution. I thought long and hard about Shauna being the one to deliver our victim impact statement. Was it a bad idea? Could I really stop her if it was something she really wanted to do? Jack was the eldest and I had relied on him a lot since the attack.

I had tried to shield Shauna and Emma from the horror of a lot of what we'd been through. But Shauna was 20 years old now and if she wanted to speak about how the attack on her dad had affected us as a family, I had to support her. We all thought about what we wanted to say, and Seán's sister Suzanne helped us put it all together. We were ready for what would most definitely be our final trip to Preston. This time we agreed that Shauna and I would travel to Preston along with Seán's sister Sinéad. Lisa, our liaison officer, informed us that it was quite likely this would be done and dusted in one day. Even though I knew this part of our journey was nearly over I found this final trip hard. I always felt Simone Mastrelli was the man responsible for doing the most damage to Seán. The father and family man, as he was described in court, was at the fore of the group of up to 60 'ultras' responsible for the attack. CCTV footage had shown him punching Seán in the side of the head. A 'single, heavy blow' as it was described. He was the man who had knocked him unconscious. He was the man who had damaged Seán's brain. After the attack Simone Mastrelli removed his balaclava and left Seán for dead. He changed his clothes and entered the stadium to watch the match. The next day he flew home to Italy. I knew as long as I lived, I would never ever be able to get my head around that level of cruelty.

We arrived back at the same courtroom in Preston Crown Court and again took our seats in the public gallery. Mastrelli had fought extradition in several appeals but had finally been brought back to the UK and here he was behind us in the courtroom. This time around there was no other family present: Mastrelli was on his own. He was sentenced to three and a half years in prison for unlawfully and maliciously inflicting grievous bodily harm on Seán. In sentencing, Judge Mark Brown said the assault was a 'dreadful offence' which had had a profound impact on Seán and his family. He went on to say it was 'particularly callous of Mastrelli to have continued on into the match'. The court was told that he had written us a letter saying he was sorry for what happened that day. I was asked if I would accept it, but I couldn't. His barrister said he was 'distraught' at the suffering he had caused. He was described as a 'good person', someone who 'had worked all of his life'. But I didn't want a letter from this man who had left my husband for dead and gone on to watch a soccer match. This wasn't his opportunity to give his side of the story: it was our opportunity to give ours.

As Shauna was about to take the stand to deliver the victim impact statement on behalf of our family, I gave her one last chance to change her mind. It was such a strange and foreign environment to be in, I wanted to make sure she wasn't having second thoughts. But she wasn't. Judge Mark Brown called her name. She stood up and made her way to the stand. She could hear Seán's voice in her head, 'Put your shoulders back, Shauna, and don't mumble, speak clearly.' She took the stand and began. 'Before this attack my dad was a fit and confident man with a passion for life who represented everything that was good in life.' Mastrelli watched on from the dock. She took her time. 'He was a mentor and a proud family man with a great community spirit. The violent and unprovoked attack left Dad in a dire situation, his future is uncertain, and we don't know how he will progress and that really frightens us.' As she read each sentence, she looked up at Mastrelli and paused. Then she continued, 'Over the past 10 months we have spent all our time at Dad's bedside and have celebrated birthdays and Christmas, when all we want is our dad to be home. We hope and pray every day to see improvement in our dad and the focus for us is on getting Dad the proper care he needs.' You could hear a pin drop in the courtroom as she finished. 'My dad went to watch his beloved team, Liverpool, and he never came home.' This was her defining moment. Shauna had wanted the victim impact statement to pack a punch and it certainly did.

One Year On

It was almost one year since the attack. Some days it felt like only yesterday and other days it felt like it had happened five years ago. Seán had good days and bad days; we all did. The reality of what had happened hit me really hard sometimes, when I least expected it. Even though a year had passed, it felt like we were really only at the starting line. We had a long road ahead of us. Our fundraising efforts, which were in full swing, were a very welcome distraction. It was hard to accept but deep down I knew I had no option but to fundraise for Seán's care. If I didn't, his limited options were going to disappear. Seán was going to need round-the-clock care for the rest of his life. I knew very early on that Seán would never work again. In The Walton Centre after the attack Professor Eldridge had warned me that Seán's injuries were 'life-changing'. Dealing with the fact that that part of his life was over was really hard. He had always been an extremely hard worker, even as a teenager when he went in search of a job in his local pub, The Steering Wheel in Clondalkin. He had wanted a job as soon as he could legally get one. In his early twenties he began his career in the electrical business when he got a job working on a trade counter at a hardware store in Clondalkin. Over the past 25 years he had worked his way up through a number of different companies and was very well known in the industry. His colleagues and former colleagues were so supportive of Seán and us as a family after the attack.

Eight months after the attack, a massive coffee morning was organised which was a very emotional affair, and not just for me. The fundraiser was the brainchild of a man called Gerry O'Sullivan from Co. Kerry. Gerry owned an electrical company, TradeKit, which is based in Ballycasheen. Seán had worked as a sales director at Precision Cables in Dundalk for about a decade before the attack. His job involved a lot of trips to Killarney and Tralee to meet clients and he and Gerry had gotten to know each other well over the years. Gerry was shocked to hear what had happened to Seán and wanted to do something to help his fellow tradesman. He had the idea to hold a coffee morning, and not just any ordinary coffee morning, but one that the whole electrical industry would get involved in. Gerry wanted to get the ball rolling so he sent off a few emails to different people to see what they thought. A week later he suffered a heart attack and very sadly passed away. Sometime after that his family were going through his affairs and they came across the emails he had sent about the coffee morning that he wanted to organise for Seán. They could have just let it go, given everything they had been through, but they didn't. Gerry's son Joe had taken the reins at the company and he was determined to see it through to honour his dad. The family felt it had been Gerry's last wish. I was so touched. They were grieving themselves so the fact that they went out of their way to do this for Seán and for us was so selfless. I later met Gerry's wife in person and it was incredibly emotional for both of us.

Seán's boss at Precision Cables, Fergus O'Callaghan, and his good friend Paul Noonan played a massive role in the success of the coffee morning. He invited us to the company's coffee morning at their offices in Dundalk, and myself, Shauna and Emma went along. It was actually really hard to walk into Seán's empty office. Fergus was really cut up when he heard the news about what had happened to Seán and had travelled to The Walton Centre to see him. Seán was extremely ambitious and good at what he did. He knew the electrical industry like the back of his hand. It had taken a massive hit during the recession and Precision Cables wasn't immune from the hard times. But they managed to weather the storm and come out the other side. I think at first Fergus hoped that Seán would eventually return to work but I knew that would never happen and eventually I met with Fergus to tell him this was the end of the road for Seán at the company.

A couple of weeks before the attack, Seán had received a new work car. The sales directors changed their cars every two years because they clocked up so much mileage travelling around Ireland meeting clients. This time Seán had decided to go for a red Audi. I don't know much about cars but it was fabulous. I remember the first day it was parked outside the house Jack came home with his girlfriend Laura. 'Whose car is that?' he said as he walked into the kitchen. I explained it was his dad's new car. He couldn't believe it. 'Is he having some sort of midlife crisis?' he asked, laughing. One of the hardest days for me over the course of this whole journey was strangely the day the car was taken away from the house. I was at home with my neighbour and friend Edel. I knew the people from Audi were coming to collect the car and I also knew I didn't have it in me to go out and hand over the keys. I felt so sad about it all. I explained to Edel that they were on their way and I asked her would she do it for me, which she did. It wasn't about the car, it was what it signified. Seán was never going to work again. His income was gone. He was also never going to drive again. It was a big reality check for me. There had always been two cars sitting in our driveway and it took me a long time to not feel a pang of sadness when I'd drive in and notice that. The red Audi was so brand new I had actually never been in it. Seán had never got round to taking me for a drive. I couldn't help but think of all the drives he had taken me on in the little red Fiat 127 we had saved for and bought the year after we first met. A different time, a different life. Seán had always been so sensible and responsible with his life plan. Get a job, meet a girl, get married, buy a house and have children. That had all worked out for him. It was only in recent years he had really started to enjoy himself a bit more. In many ways he had achieved a lot of what he had set out to do and now it was time for him to take it a bit easier. He enjoyed his sport and a few pints, his golfing outings and our holidays. It felt like such a loss that the rug was pulled from under him at a time in his life that he would have enjoyed so much.

At this stage plans were afoot for the charity match in Seán's honour at the Aviva Stadium in Dublin. The seeds had been sown for this at the first meeting between the chairman of the Seán Cox Rehabilitation Trust, Stephen

Felle, and the CEO of Liverpool FC, Peter Moore. Stephen and Peter had stayed in regular contact since their first meeting. They spoke the same language and had started to develop a friendship. Months of planning and organising had taken place and a date was set. On 12 April 2019 a team of Liverpool legends led by Kenny Dalglish was to take on an Ireland side managed by Mick McCarthy to raise money for Seán's rehab. Seán's two sporting loves were coming together at the Aviva. As the date drew closer I got it into my head that I wanted to try to get Seán to the Aviva for the match. Seán had missed so many milestones over the previous year; he wasn't missing this one. But he hadn't been out of hospital in almost a year. He'd spent over four weeks in The Walton Centre in Liverpool followed by almost five months in Beaumont Hospital before his transfer to the NRH.

I knew it would be a big challenge logistically to get him there, but I had to at least try. I asked the advice of his medical team and they told me they didn't see why he couldn't go, once the right supports were put in place. They agreed to allow Seán more rest time in the days before the match so he could conserve his energy and they also suggested that two staff members accompany us to make sure Seán was comfortable. I started to get excited about the prospect of getting him out of a medical setting for the first time in a year. The fact it was to watch a soccer match involving some of his sporting heroes was the icing on the cake. I was nervous too though. Seán had always had medical help on hand if he needed it: what if something went wrong? Then again, what if it didn't? I began to plan the outing meticulously. I asked Fergus McNulty for his help. His brother Niall, who also works at Marymount Care Centre, had access to a wheelchair-accessible vehicle. He agreed to transport Seán from the NRH to the Aviva. Paul, an occupational therapist, from St Peter's GAA Club, and Joan, a carer from Marymount Care Centre, also agreed to come with us. Our plans were in place.

I started to talk to Seán about the upcoming match. I told him who was going to be there and I showed him photographs of the tickets and the posters advertising the event. I found this part hard. I wanted Seán to know this was being done for him, but I also wanted to remain positive and upbeat around him. I didn't want him to know we had to fundraise because he had been injured. This was a tricky one for me, and it still is. Over the previous months we had started to use a whiteboard to help Seán to communicate. We wrote little messages on it and encouraged him to do the same. One of the nights I was visiting Seán and his friend Paul Pilkington was in the bed opposite him. They were keeping each other company as they always did. I whispered to Seán that we should ask Paul to come to the match with us, so we got the whiteboard and wrote on it, 'Want to come to the Aviva?' Seán held it up and we called Paul's name. He was absolutely thrilled. The two of them were getting a night out. It was such a lovely moment. They had become close friends at this stage and it just wouldn't have felt right heading off to the Aviva without him. It gave the pair of them such a lift.

But before we got to the Aviva, I had to find myself a dress. Shopping for clothes, something I'd done routinely in the past, now seemed like such an odd thing to have to do. I hadn't had time to give any thought to what I was wearing since the attack – I'd been pretty much living in one hospital or another for the past year. And now I needed to find a dress suitable for a black-tie event. It felt like going from nought to sixty. A gala dinner at the Intercontinental Hotel in Ballsbridge in Dublin had been organised for the night before the match. More than 600 tickets had been sold for the event which was also going to be attended by the Liverpool and Ireland footballers playing in the match along with a host of other famous faces. A charity auction was to take place and a Liverpool jersey signed by Mo Salah and a round of golf with Jamie Redknapp were two of the items on offer. One of Seán's favourite singers, Mundy, was going to perform while comedy on the night would be provided by Mario Rosenstock. RTÉ broadcasters Claire Byrne and Darragh Maloney were on hosting duties. And I was to do an onstage interview. I was nervous. Speaking in public like this was something I had been on quite a journey with over the previous year. Seán's injury put us as a family in the public eye and I found it really hard to accept that. I have always been naturally quite shy and being the centre of attention is just something I'm not comfortable with. Speaking in public didn't come easily to me. I had no problem giving presentations in a work setting on a topic I was comfortable and confident speaking about – if I could prepare for whatever it was I had to do I was fine. But speaking about Seán was different. It always felt like I was sharing something that wasn't mine to share, and it made me feel very sad. But as the months went on I realised it was a necessary part of the journey if I wanted Seán to get the help he needed.

There was an interest in Seán's story, people were disgusted that he had been so badly injured in such a vicious attack, and people were always curious to know how he was doing. I've never become fully comfortable in these settings but I suppose I got better at handling them. I've always made sure to make my boundaries very clear before doing any interviews and that's always been respected. I also knew that speaking about Seán afforded me an opportunity to thank people. We had been on the receiving end of such an outpouring of love and support over the previous year. I wasn't just Seán's voice to advocate for better care, I was also his voice to say 'Thank you'. It was important to me that people knew how much we appreciated what they had done. I thought back to the conversation Seán had had with Fergus McNulty when he was trying to convince him to take on the role of chairman at St Peter's GAA Club. He had been so honest with him about how the part of the job that involved making speeches or being centre stage wasn't something that came easily to him. But he was motivated by a deep love for the GAA and St Peter's. If Seán could dig deep and do it for the club then I could do it for Seán. And I knew that if the shoe was on the other foot, Seán would do it for me.

I had very little time to find a dress with everything involved in preparing Seán for the Aviva, but I got there in the end. My instinct was to buy a black dress, which made me laugh as Seán had always hated me wearing black. I wore a lot of black to work and he used to tease me. 'Are you going to a funeral or what?' he'd say. He loved when I wore anything colourful. When I saw this gold dress I knew it was 'the one'. I was sure if Seán had been there he would have given it his seal of approval. I arrived at the hotel with the two girls, Emma and Shauna. We were shown an area we could use to get ready. When we walked in Claire Byrne was also in there getting ready. I had met her before when I was interviewed on the *Claire Byrne Live* show so I knew she'd put me at ease during the interview. It was an incredibly emotional night. Liverpool legends Kenny Dalglish and Ian Rush mingled with the likes of Mick McCarthy, Robbie Keane, Jason McAteer and Phil Babb. The room was bursting with love and support as pictures and videos of Seán were shown on a big screen.

A few weeks before the event, Seán had made a bit of a breakthrough with his efforts to speak. He had started to say a few words, when prompted. We decided to try to record a video of him saying 'thank you'. It took a number of attempts, but we got there in the end. When Seán appeared in his wheelchair on the big screen you could hear a pin drop in the room. Hundreds of people looked on as he gave a thumbs-up and quietly said the words, 'Thank you.' There wasn't a dry eye in the house. It had been Seán's birthday a few days beforehand so in a way it felt like we were having a big party for him. But of course he wasn't there. Jack, Shauna and Emma surrounded me at our table. Seán's brothers and sisters were there with their wives and husbands, as was my family and so many of our close friends. I remember looking around the big, fancy room and feeling overwhelmed by the love we had been shown over the past 12 months from people we knew, and from complete strangers too. I don't know how we would have survived that first year without it. It was so heartwarming. But my heart was also aching. I really missed Seán. Everyone was there with someone – Jack even had his girlfriend Laura there with him – but I was on my own. Seán was so sociable. He would have adored a night like that with all of his sporting and entertainment heroes in one room. It felt like such a loss. I was surrounded by people, so I certainly wasn't alone, but I was lonely.

Tea With Michael D.

The following day I made my way up Lansdowne Road to the Aviva Stadium in a taxi. From the window I could see fans of all ages making their way to the match. Some wore red, some wore green, some wore half scarves bearing both the Ireland and Liverpool crests. Almost 27,000 people had bought tickets for the match. I guess it was an opportunity for people to see their heroes in action, even if some of them were past their prime. It was also an opportunity for people to help Seán, which they were doing in their thousands. It still took my breath away that so many people were willing to support us in that way. Seán's obsession with soccer hadn't rubbed off on me over the years but I was really looking forward to the match. Knowing Seán was going to be there too made all the difference for me. I had struggled the night before at the gala dinner. I had really felt Seán's absence and it really hurt. But he was going to be with us today. I was shown to the VIP area of the Aviva by security to wait for Seán. I just couldn't settle until I saw him.

I didn't have to wait too long as moments later he arrived safely from the NRH. I felt calmer; everything was going to be okay. Sir Kenny Dalglish and Liverpool FC CEO, Peter Moore, came to say hello to us. Seán's face was a sight to behold when he saw King Kenny. There was no doubt he knew exactly who he was. We had done all we could to make sure he was safe and comfortable for the match. The room was spacious, with big screens mounted on the walls. There was also a big glass window looking down on the pitch. A few of the players asked could they come and meet Seán before the match. He may not have been able to verbalise what he was thinking but I knew how happy he was. He was taking it all in. Speaking to the media afterwards former Liverpool and Ireland midfielder Jason McAteer said, 'I got to see Seán before the game, and it broke my heart. It could have happened to anyone, any one of us. It's like sliding doors, isn't it? A minute later, 10 minutes before.' He was so right. That was something I had thought about a lot over the previous year. What if Seán and Marty had been five minutes longer eating their dinner? What if they had decided to go into the stadium 10 minutes later? What if they'd taken a different route? Could this have been avoided? Too many what-ifs to contemplate.

The children and I had been asked to go out onto the pitch with President Michael D. Higgins before kickoff, so when the time came, we made our way down to the bowels of the Aviva to get ready. After Seán had been attacked, President Higgins had written to me to tell me he had been saddened and appalled to hear about what had happened to Seán and that 'the many tributes that have been paid during the past week speak of a man who is held in the highest regard and affection within the community'. He wished me and the children the best and said himself and his wife Sabina would keep Seán in their thoughts. Down in the tunnel area of the Aviva we were shown to a formal table with a crisp white tablecloth. Tea and coffee were being poured from silver pots into china cups as President Higgins made his way over to us. He told us how sorry he was about what had happened, and I introduced Jack, Shauna and Emma to him. He was lovely. As we waited to go out onto the pitch, we just sat there making small talk with the president. At one stage one of the kids kicked me under the table, their way of saying, 'What do I say to the president?' It was another very surreal moment for all of us and one we never imagined we'd find ourselves in. The players made their way out onto the pitch and we followed. A minute's silence was held to mark the 30th anniversary of the Hillsborough disaster which was a few days later. As soon as it ended, a rousing rendition of 'You'll Never Walk Alone' began to sweep through the stadium. I stood in the middle of the pitch looking up at all the people in the stands. It felt so strange to be there. We were just a normal family, we had always been a normal family. We had never ever wanted for anything in life only to be content and healthy and together. That was it. That was the dream as far as we were concerned. And now here we were in this situation. The hair was standing on the back of my neck. I felt so emotional.

People knew who Seán was now, who we were. We never wanted that. But I knew ultimately it would help Seán. It would mean I could get him the help he needed. I was so moved that all these people were here for Seán. He had stared evil in the face the night he was attacked but as the crowds got to the chorus, *walk on … walk on … with hope in your heart,* I was struck by how much good there is in the world too. Many people had shown Seán their support because they felt what happened to him could happen to anyone. He was a decent man doing something he loved, something he had done hundreds of times before. Thousands more were motivated to support Seán by their affinity to Liverpool FC. I thought back on the way I had felt after my first meeting with Peter Moore. I'd doubted his commitment to Seán. I'd thought they might support us for a few months and then forget all about us. But Peter had kept his word. Between the money raised at the match, the gala dinner the night before and the donation from the first team players, Liverpool had helped us raise €748,000 for Seán's care. I knew we would have never raised that amount of money if Liverpool hadn't thrown its weight behind us. But it was more than that. Peter Moore stayed in contact with both me and Stephen Felle via text messages and emails. He wanted us to know the club was willing to walk this road with Seán. They felt he was one of them. It is a global corporation, but one with a heart. The match was a lively affair even though some of the players may have been a bit rusty. They put on a great performance, interacting with the spectators, and the crowd loved it. But the man everyone was really there to see only made one appearance. It came 22 minutes into the game when Seán's face flashed up on the big screen in the stadium watching the match closely from his seat. Everyone was on their feet cheering and clapping. Liverpool won 2–1 but everyone went home happy. It was a special day, and one none of us will ever forget.

A Very Lonely Road

ealising there was no clear pathway for Seán in the country where he had been born, and spent all his working life contributing to, was a bitter pill to swallow. Life was hard enough without having to up sticks and move to another country. Our life was in Ireland, our children were here, our friends were here, and of course our support network was here. I was so daunted by the idea of travelling this road in another country on my own. I knew if I had to do it for Seán I would, but I wished there was another option. At this stage we had ruled out travelling to Germany for rehab, as young Pádraig Schaler who had been injured in the US had done. This wasn't going to be possible for Seán. I had visited a facility for people with acquired brain injuries in Mountbolus in Offaly which had been suggested to me. It was a campus with 30 beds spread out in different houses, with a shared kitchen, dining and reception area. I didn't feel it ticked all the boxes in terms of what Seán needed, though, so I began to think about trying to find a rehab centre in the UK. I guessed there were probably a lot of options, but I was going to have to really do my research to make sure I found the right one. I mentioned the UK as an option to Professor Delargy at the NRH. I was hoping he may have some knowledge to impart or even a steer in the right direction. He warned me to keep my money and said I shouldn't be fooled by some of the promises made by rehab centres in the UK.

In the meantime a meeting had been arranged to discuss Seán's move to The Royal Hospital Donnybrook. Professor Delargy said he had spoken to the people at the hospital and it was an option for Seán to go there until we knew what we might do in the long-term. Again, he reiterated that Donnybrook was a step-down facility and Seán would not be receiving as much rehab as he was at the NRH. But at least it would buy me some time to make sure I made the right decision for Seán. I was so relieved I didn't have to make a massive decision like that in a rush. I really wanted to make sure I found the most suitable place for Seán's specific needs – I was desperate to give him the best possible chance. A multidisciplinary meeting was arranged to discuss Seán's move from the NRH to Donnybrook. It was held in Dún Laoghaire and attended by Professor Delargy and Dr Paul Carroll from The Royal Hospital Donnybrook. Three of Seán's siblings, Peter, Marty and Suzanne, came with me as did his cousin Richard. Since the attack on Seán I have had to make so many big decisions about his care. I have had to speak for him and fight for him. I have had to make sure people didn't give up on him. Before the attack, myself and Seán worked together on life's big decisions – we were a real team in that way. Being on my own felt so daunting but Seán's brothers and sisters have really stepped up. We have made all the big decisions about Seán together; I've always consulted with them and asked their advice on different parts of the journey. They've always been so willing to do whatever they could to help me and I honestly don't know what I would have done without them.

The five of us entered the room together where we met with all of the people who had been working with Seán at the NRH over the previous months: his occupational therapist, physiotherapist and speech and language therapists and their equivalents at The Royal Hospital Donnybrook. As I entered the room, I was struck by how many people were now involved in Seán's life. It was one of those strange reality check moments. I was introduced to Dr Carroll, who chatted to me about Donnybrook and how to find the car park if Seán became a patient there. We took our seats around a big table. Before long the various medics and therapists introduced themselves and outlined their work with Seán: how he had been on arrival from Beaumont Hospital, the progress he had made since, and his daily nursing and care needs. The meeting was long and detailed with a lot of information flying back and forth. I had to answer a lot of questions about Seán and his future, some of which I found very difficult. As it came to an end Dr Carroll spoke first. 'I don't think we can take him,' he said.

There was silence in the room. I looked around the table at Seán's family. None of us had been expecting this. He went on to say that he hadn't realised how substantial Seán's nursing needs were or how complex the case was, and for that reason Donnybrook would probably not be suitable. I looked over at Professor Delargy. We had been led to believe that Donnybrook had already agreed to take Seán. The atmosphere in the room became very tense. Dr Carroll said he would hold off on making a final decision for the moment. He said he would check on the possibility of having extra nursing resources commissioned to look after Seán to ensure his safety. But it was too little, too late. I knew Seán was never going to Donnybrook. None of it made sense to me. Why hadn't Seán been assessed first, before this multidisciplinary team meeting had been called? How had I been given the impression that this was a done deal? I was really upset. The team from Donnybrook left the room and I turned to Professor Delargy. 'What happens to Seán now?' I asked. 'Well he'll have to go back to where he came from,' he replied. I stood up and gathered my notes. Two weeks later I got a call to confirm what I already knew: there was no place for Seán in Donnybrook.

What was I going to do now? I had no plan B. I didn't think I needed one. I thought about Pádraig Schaler's parents and how they had warned us when we met them that people with brain injuries walk a very lonely road in this country. How right they had been. It wasn't an option for me to hop on a plane to the UK to try to find somewhere for Seán to go. Emma was preparing to do her Leaving Cert; I wasn't going to leave her again. I spoke to our social worker about how unhappy I was with the sequence of events and with how everything had been communicated. As a family, we had been on such a rollercoaster since the attack. This uncertainty was the last thing we needed. It felt like the people in charge had absolutely no understanding or empathy for what it feels like to have someone you love injured so badly you cannot bring them home. I had shared a life with Seán for 30 years – how could I sleep at night if I didn't know what path he was on? It wasn't an option to just sit back and see what happened or take each day at a time. At no point was it going to be possible for me to put Seán into my car and just drive him back to the safety of our home. He was too ill for that, so I had to have a plan for him. I had no issue with the fact that Donnybrook wasn't suitable for Seán. If they couldn't meet his needs, then I was glad he wasn't going there. But what really annoyed me was the fact that it was all so avoidable.

I later received an apology from The Royal Hospital Donnybrook. In August 2019 Dr Carroll wrote to me to clarify that he had never made any commitment to take Seán as a patient prior to the meeting. He wrote, 'It may also be helpful to clarify that the Royal Hospital Donnybrook service had not accepted Seán prior to the meeting. I understand that the NRH may have given you to understand that Seán could go to Royal Hospital Donnybrook. However, the decision around admissions is decided by Donnybrook and not the NRH.' In my correspondence with the social worker, I pointed out how disappointed I was with how everything had been handled and I urged her to see if it could be improved in the future for other people in the same situation as us. In his letter Dr Carroll had also written, 'I am aware that an apology has been given to you from the NRH … You asked that this aspect of communication between Donnybrook and the NRH be improved and I can advise that such work is in the early stages of development and your feedback will be very helpful to move this forward.' At least this was something. I don't know if the process for transferring people from the NRH to The Royal Hospital Donnybrook has improved but I'd like to think it has and that no other family will have to suffer the uncertainty of not knowing where their loved one will end up next.

The NRH offered to extend Seán's stay until Emma completed her Leaving Cert. I accepted the offer because I had no other option but the last three months of Seán's time there was a challenge. Almost immediately I noticed a change in Seán's programme of daily rehab. He was doing much less physio and speech and language therapy. I couldn't understand what was going on, so I asked. The explanation I was given was that this can happen as it approaches summer with staff taking their annual leave. I thought this was so unfair. People only get one shot at the NRH. What if you're unlucky enough to be admitted in the summertime when people were on holiday? Would you get a better level of care if you could choose the winter months? Was the quality of rehab on offer in Ireland potluck? Seán wasn't being stimulated as much as he had been, and as a result he became quite agitated. I'd often arrive to visit him to find him with his head down and in bad form. It was very unlike him. He had an iPad to watch but even that was difficult for him because of the trouble with his eyesight. It was really hard to witness. We all spent many evenings just trying to pick him up and improve his mood before we had to leave him again for the night. My fear was that all the hard work he had put in would be lost; he had built up so much strength over the previous months, I didn't want him to go backwards in his recovery.

A few months later when the time came for Seán to leave the NRH I received Professor Delargy's discharge report. It outlined the journey Seán had been on from arriving at The Walton Hospital with 'an acute subdural haematoma traumatic subarachnoid haemorrhage 11mm in depth with 13mm midline shift. He was very ill at the time with respiratory sepsis'. It went on to detail how Seán had arrived from Beaumont Hospital to the NRH 'in a minimally conscious state and has emerged in a much more interactive state'. All correct. But as I read on, I came to a paragraph that read, 'Some frustration had emerged for Seán in recent weeks which is understandable given his emerging insight and awareness and his incomplete neurological recovery. Unfortunately, there has not been as much improvement in his mobility or communication in the past six weeks or so … he shows clear evidence at this stage of enjoying the more social aspects of life rather than intensive rehabilitation sessions.' I was disappointed. This implied that Seán was refusing rehab. I only wished he was capable of such a thing. He had a severe brain injury and he was far from consistent with his commands. The first word that had come back to him was 'yeah' and as a result he relied on it a lot. Sadly, he wasn't yet able to express a preference for one thing over another and yet the implication in his discharge report was that he was choosing not to partake in therapy.

I called the social worker and told her the discharge report did not accurately represent what had happened during Seán's last few weeks at the NRH. I told her I wanted it changed. She explained that discharge reports are never altered. 'Even if they're wrong?' I asked. I wouldn't drop it.

It wasn't right. Eventually it was changed and returned to me. The NRH offered an extension of Seán's stay, but it was bed and breakfast and an evening meal. The NRH suffered because Seán was now taking up a bed earmarked for someone else. I suffered because I felt backed into a corner with nowhere to escape to. But most of all Seán suffered. We left the NRH disappointed that a journey that had begun so positively was ending this way.

The Next STEP

Rehab in the UK was now Seán's best and only option. If I was to give Seán the best chance of recovery, we were going to have to leave the country, so my next job was to try to find the best place for him to go. It was recommended we employ the services of a case manager who would help us source the type of rehab we were looking for so that's what we did. Elaine O'Flaherty came over to meet Seán at the NRH to assess exactly what he needed and then she set about drawing up a short list for me. I spent hours navigating my way through the websites of different rehab facilities. I looked at the pictures to see if I could imagine Seán being happy there, making the progress I so badly wanted him to make. I investigated what kind of therapies were on offer. I read about how qualified the staff were and what was on the dinner menu. But for me the biggest deciding factor was something you can't get a sense of from a website. I wanted to know what the atmosphere was like. As Seán had become more alert over the previous months, I was struck many times by how important his environment was to him. I needed to know more about the ethos of these centres; was hope, optimism and positivity encouraged? That was what we needed the most for this next chapter of Seán's journey.

I decided I'd have to visit these places myself to get a feel for them; I'd have to see them with my own eyes. With the help of Elaine, I arranged several visits to find the most suitable place for Seán. I asked Seán's sister, Sinéad, and Marie, one of the nurses from Marymount Care Centre in Lucan, to come with myself and Elaine. Between the four of us I knew we'd find the place most suitable for Seán's needs. Over the course of two trips we visited several different rehab centres, some of them amazing and others I could rule out immediately. As we walked through the door of one of them Sinéad tried to grab my arm and steer me straight back out. We all knew immediately it wasn't the right place. On another occasion we were met by an accountant who showed us around the facility. He never mentioned Seán's injuries or enquired about his needs. We left that one knowing we wouldn't be back. And then there was STEPS Rehabilitation in Sheffield. Again, this was a case of 'when you know, you know'. It was the very first facility we visited and from the minute we walked in I got a good feeling. I still remember pulling up outside the modern building on Troutbeck Road which looked down a hill. It almost seemed out of sync with its surroundings, probably because it was a purpose-built facility. Two sisters, Jules Leahy and Toria Chan, opened the centre in May 2017. They had both worked in the National Health Service in the UK and had a wealth of medical experience between them. Their mission was to help those with life-changing injuries and illnesses to achieve their full potential. They offered rehab to people recovering from brain and spine injuries, strokes and complex trauma injuries.

When we arrived, we were met by a member of the team who showed us around. On the ground floor there was a reception area, a big spacious café and an exit to a beautiful garden. There was also a large therapy gym and a hydrotherapy pool on that floor. They even had a little hairdresser where clients could get their hair done, a games room and a music room. There were 23 rooms across two levels, each with its own bathroom and television. I remember noticing the smallest of details, like the nice comfortable-looking armchair in each room for visitors. I knew I'd spend most of my time sitting with Seán. The range of therapies on offer was extensive. There was all the usual stuff on the list like occupational therapy, speech and language and physiotherapy. But there were also therapies that were new to me: a sensory programme, voice skills classes and neuro-stimulation therapy. But most importantly the atmosphere appealed to me from the minute we walked in. It struck me how happy the staff walking around seemed to be. They were smiling and chatting to the people around them who were referred to as clients and not patients. They all wore different-coloured polo shirts so it didn't feel like we were in a medical setting. It was homely and there was a definite air of positivity about the place, which I felt we really needed at this stage. The four of us loved it but we kept our counsel until we had visited all the rehab facilities on our list. Once we ticked off every place we each announced our personal preference. And it was a unanimous decision: Seán was going to STEPS. It was going to come at a huge cost but I was hopeful he'd make some progress. I knew a minimum stay of 12 weeks was needed for any real benefits to be seen so I booked him in for three months to see what gains he might achieve.

This of course meant I was also moving to Sheffield. Again Elaine, our case manager, helped enormously with this, and set about finding me a place to live. We communicated via email as I just didn't have the time to travel over and back to view different options. My hands were full preparing Seán for what was happening next. I told Elaine my only criteria were to be as close to STEPS as possible and to have a second bed so people from Ireland could visit. I knew I was going to spend most of my day with Seán so I was hoping I could walk back and forth and not have to get taxis or public transport. I also knew Jack, Shauna and Emma and Seán's family and my family would want to visit so having a spare room would mean people could stay with me. Thankfully Elaine managed to find the perfect place for me, an Airbnb that ticked all the boxes. It was a two-bedroomed apartment 10 minutes' walk from Seán. It was such a relief to know what was happening next after all the uncertainty over where Seán would go after the National Rehabilitation Hospital. But now I had to face the fact that I was also moving to Sheffield for at least three months and leaving the children again.

Emma was still only 18. She had just finished her Leaving Cert and had accepted a place at Dublin Institute of Technology in September. I was worried about her. Her dad had been missing from her life for the best part of a year and a half at that stage and starting college can be such an adjustment for so many teenagers. Jack was 23 and was going into his third and final year of Construction Studies, also at Dublin Institute of Technology, and Shauna, who was 22, would be starting her second year in Early Childhood Education at Marino Institute of Education. Not only were they going to be left on their own but they also needed to move out of our house to allow the builders to move in. Our house was going to have to be remodelled if we wanted our dream of getting Seán home to become a reality. The plan was for Seán to come home full time at the start of 2020 so we needed to make sure it was both safe and comfortable for him. It had to be made fully wheelchair-accessible and we needed to install specialist medical equipment. I also knew we'd need a bedroom and bathroom downstairs for Seán. It was a big job, a lot of work needed to be done, and as I approached the project I felt so overwhelmed by it. Part of the joy of being married or in a long-term relationship is sharing the burden and excitement of these big life moments with someone. Myself and Seán always worked so well together so I felt like I was very much on my own when it came to knowing what needed to be done with the house. I decided to ask Niall McNulty from Marymount Care Centre to help me. I knew that he had recently overseen the building of an extension at the nursing home, and that he would know exactly what I needed to do. I was right and thankfully Niall jumped right into the project with me. He accompanied me to various meetings and offered his advice and expertise on all aspects of making a home comfortable and safe for someone in a wheelchair. His help was invaluable to me.

Once we had our plans in place, I knew that when Seán would eventually come home he would certainly have everything he needed from a medical point of view. Niall's support during the process also made me feel much less alone. The house was going to take months to complete so it made sense to let the builders move in when Seán was in Sheffield. So, I set about finding the children a house to rent. This proved much harder than I expected. I wanted them to be able to remain in Dunboyne because that was where they were most familiar with and I knew all our close friends in the village would look out for them. We were hoping the work on our house would be finished by January 2020 and we could move in then. Short-term lets were very hard to come by and I was getting to the stage where I didn't really know what I was going to do. I put the word out that we were looking for a house to rent and finally we got lucky with a woman who used to teach Emma when she was in Junior Infants in primary school. She had a cosy three-bedroom house in Dunboyne to rent and she was more than happy for us to take it. The relief. Things were finally coming together.

Like most Irish mammies I had done a lot for the kids growing up, probably too much, and now they had to fend for themselves. Ironically it was around this time that I was contacted by the organisers of the Mum of the Year awards. It's an annual event held in Dublin to recognise and celebrate the achievements of women around the country. I was asked if I would accept the Courage Award. Emma had just finished her Leaving Cert so the two of us and Seán's sister, Sinéad, went along to the awards ceremony. It was really emotional for both of us to hear the stories of all of the amazing women in the room. I was touched to be receiving the award but deep down I wished I wasn't. That was the way I always felt when we'd find ourselves in an unusual situation. 'This is great,' I'd say to myself, 'but I wish it wasn't happening and we were back living our old life that no one had any interest in.' Jack, Shauna and Emma had grown up so much since the attack and I knew they would manage fine without me but it still felt wrong to be leaving them. Shauna was as fond of a rota as I am so she was the organiser. She wrote a list of chores that needed to be done and divided them up between the three of them. I think the girls found it hard to get Jack to empty the dishwasher but they managed the things that matter the most and thankfully they all looked out for one another. We were almost ready to go but first I had to figure out how I was going to get Seán to Sheffield. Logistically it was impossible to navigate Dublin Airport. I asked Stephen Felle for his advice and he told me to leave it with him for a few days.

Stephen knew a businessman who had a private plane so he decided to ask him if he would fly Seán to Sheffield. He said he'd be delighted to help. He invited us to see the plane and make sure it was suitable for Seán. It was perfect. Our plans were in place.

On 3 September 2019 we were ready to embark on our journey to Sheffield. Leaving Dunboyne that day for the next chapter of Seán's recovery was very emotional. The plane was small so only me and Jack could travel with him. Shauna and Emma came to wave us off, along with Peter and Sinéad and their families. I hugged the girls tightly. It was so hard to say goodbye. Just like the time I had left them at home to be by Seán's bedside at The Walton Centre in Liverpool, I couldn't help but feel that I was abandoning them. I knew they'd be visiting us regularly in Sheffield, but I still felt really sad about it. They were moving into a rented house with no mam or dad around for the next three months. It was also really tough on Seán's family. They had been so committed to him while he was in Beaumont Hospital and the National Rehabilitation Hospital, spending hours by his bedside, doing everything they could to bring him along the road to recovery. And now Seán had to leave the country to get the rehabilitation he so badly needed. They also had plans to visit us, but I knew they were going to miss seeing Seán so regularly. Watching him being lifted onto the plane was so hard for all of us. He looked so vulnerable and helpless as Jack and Peter hoisted him up into his seat. I sat in beside him with Jack facing both of us. We had arranged for our luggage to be sent by courier to STEPS. I settled myself into my plush leather seat on this fancy plane with cream carpet on the floor and wondered how we had ended up here.

Almost exactly a year ago, Seán had been admitted to the National Rehabilitation Hospital in Dún Laoghaire. So much had happened in the past 12 months. 'What might this year bring?' I wondered to myself. I felt such mixed emotions. I was sad and anxious about leaving home and heading for the unknown. Would I cope without the support I had so readily available to me in Ireland, from friends and family? I would be on my own a lot more than I had been up to this point. And yet at the same time I felt hopeful about what this trip might mean for Seán. This was the intensive round-the-clock brain therapy he needed. It was the best thing for him. I closed my eyes and took a deep breath, in through my nose and out through my mouth. As the plane began to climb I reminded myself that in a few months' time we would all be at home together in our own house. Our family would be reunited. Little white clouds flew past the window as we went higher and higher into the sky. It was a beautiful sunny September day, but the wind was strong. A bump brought me back to reality. 'Nothing to worry about,' I told myself. I'd experienced many rough take-offs over the years. Within minutes it got much worse. The plane started to rock from side to side.

Jack, who was sitting facing Seán, began to smile at him, his way of telling him everything was okay. He gave him a thumbs-up, but Seán lifted his arm and returned a thumbs-down. 'Oh no,' I thought, 'he's not happy.' I turned to look at him and saw his face was turning red. He looked uncomfortable. I thought he was having a heart attack. And then he started to vomit violently. It was terrifying. Because of his mobility issues he couldn't position himself properly, so he was really struggling. It looked like he was choking so I tried to push him forward slightly. I had planned this trip meticulously, every moment of our journey from Marymount Care Centre to the front door of STEPS, with as little effort or hassle for Seán as possible. He suffered a lot from fatigue, and I didn't want him to have to spend his first few precious days in STEPS recovering from the journey over. I had pre-empted all sorts of different challenges we might encounter, but I hadn't pre-empted this. We weren't prepared at all. We tried to clean up the vomit. But the plane's lovely cream carpet was beyond rescue. Eventually Seán's stomach settled, and we calmed down. Less than an hour after we took off from Dunboyne we landed in Sheffield, but it felt like we had travelled a much longer distance. The pilot got a shock when he opened the door of the plane and saw Seán. The colour had completely drained from his face. Myself and Jack weren't much better. He had frightened the life out of us. As we sat there on the runway, with the fresh air coming in the door, I prayed I had made the right decision to bring Seán to Sheffield. Things could only get better.

A Cathartic Camino

J ust over a week later I bizarrely found myself on a plane again. This time I was on my way to Spain. Before the attack on Seán myself and my two sisters Bernie and Catherine had booked a week-long trip to walk the Camino in Spain. It was one of those trips you talk about doing for years on end and then finally someone says, 'Okay – we're doing it.' I had so many reasons in my head not to go. It was totally understandable for me to pull out of it with everything that was going on. Seán was just settling into STEPS, I now technically lived in Sheffield, the builders had moved into our home in Dunboyne and the children were living in a rented house, on their own. How could I now go to Spain for a week and leave Seán in Sheffield? The kids really wanted me to go. It was now almost a year and a half since Seán had been attacked and I had done nothing but be at his bedside, from The Walton Centre in Liverpool to Beaumont Hospital and then on to the National Rehabilitation Hospital. We were now about to start a new chapter at STEPS in Sheffield. I had returned to work when Seán was in the NRH but I had to take more time off to be with him in Sheffield. Apart from the mornings I'd been working in Dunnes Stores, I'd been with Seán every step of the way. Everyone else had had some sort of a break over the previous 18 months so Jack, Shauna and Emma convinced me to go. In fact, the children had always been the ones to remind me that if I didn't look after myself, I wouldn't be able to look after Seán.

I remember about five months after the attack I hadn't as much as gone for a walk when the three of them intervened. Seán and I had been members of a local fitness group called Fit4Life which was held at Dunboyne Athletic Club. Every Tuesday and Thursday evening we'd head down together and through the gates. He would go his way and meet the lads and I'd go my way and meet the girls and then when we had our exercise done, we'd walk back out together. When the children were younger, we were always so busy ferrying them to training, matches, dance classes and competitions, this was something just for us. When the children encouraged me to get back to some exercise, I just knew I could never go back. How would I walk through those gates and meet the girls when Seán was lying in a hospital bed? But I had enjoyed the camaraderie of exercising with a group and I knew I'd get more from it than just going for a walk or a run on my own. I decided I'd at least try to go back. The first time, I bottled it at the gate and turned on my heel and went home. The second attempt also failed but on my third go I made it through the gate. The friends I had made were all there and they were delighted to see me, but it was honestly one of the hardest things I've done. Now here I was contemplating going to Spain. Could I really go? The decision was made much easier when Seán's brother Peter and his wife, Aisling, offered to fly to Sheffield to spend the whole week with Seán while I was gone so I knew I didn't have to worry about him. In hindsight it was the best thing for me and the best thing for Seán.

I guess when you're running on a treadmill you don't pay too much attention to what's happening around you but then when you stop it hits you like a ton of bricks. I was exhausted from everything we'd been through. It was a physical exhaustion and a mental one too. Some people I'm sure would have prescribed a week lying on a sun lounger by a pool but I knew that wouldn't work for me. I needed a break, but I also needed something else to focus on and walking the Camino was the perfect solution. The three of us spent the next week walking, talking and laughing. People had advised me to bring headphones so I could listen to music as I walked. I brought them alright, but I never once used them. We just talked and talked and talked as we walked. Every day we'd cover about 27 miles from one town to the next. We'd stop at little cafés for a coffee and some lunch before moving on to the next spot. I always kept my phone with me, but we didn't always have Wi-Fi, so I had no choice but to switch off for short periods of time. At night we'd have dinner and a glass of wine and then collapse into bed, ready to do it all again the next day. We met lots of different groups of people along the way, but we mostly kept ourselves to ourselves. We never told anyone why we were there, and I didn't talk about Seán's story at all. I think in hindsight it was exactly what I needed.

I returned to Sheffield with a renewed energy to help Seán through the next steps of his recovery. He had already settled in well. I was so pleased to see the staff and therapists seemed to have already got the measure of Seán. 'Coxy, time for your physio!' I heard one of them say as I made my way back in to see Seán. They had started to address him by his nickname. 'Coxy' was what Seán's nearest and dearest called him over the years, and he loved it. The people working at STEPS knew how passionate Seán was about sport and how much he loved anything to do with Liverpool FC. They quickly started to use sport as a tool to reach Seán and encourage him to engage with all the therapies on offer. They put a huge amount of effort into getting to know Seán. While I had been in Spain, he had been introduced to the different people who would be working with him. They had assessed him and drawn up a plan for his rehab for the next 12 weeks.

I was encouraged by some of the small changes they were making to his routine. When Seán had been in the NRH, he had always been showered in the morning time. Due to all his mobility issues this would take a lot out of him and leave him really fatigued for the rest of the day, which obviously had an impact on how well he could manage his different therapies. STEPS realised this very quickly and decided they were going to start showering Seán at nighttime instead. Such a small change but it had a massive impact on his general wellbeing during each day. Very quickly Seán got into a routine of therapy. Every morning began with a sensory programme. The therapy involved a focus being placed on Seán's left side, which had been badly damaged in the attack. The therapist used different materials like cotton wool, a toothbrush or a spiky ball to stimulate the nerves and the muscles on his weak side. They'd get the toothbrush and run it in between each one of his fingers, slowly and then faster; they'd press it firmly down and then they'd do it lightly. They'd run the spiky ball up and down his left arm using different pressures and different speeds. It was all about using different materials and different techniques to improve the feeling in his arm. The therapy ended with Seán having oil massaged into his hands and arms and he loved it. The whole process was repeated at nighttime. They also worked on the pain Seán had been left with in his left shoulder through a therapy called neuro stimulation. After two sessions Seán was encouraged to rest before moving on to the next thing. This meant he never got too tired and was able to make it through everything on his programme.

All the clients ate together in the breakfast room and the dining room. This was significant for me, and quite emotional, as since Seán's attack he had only ever eaten behind a curtain with a nurse. Now here he was eating with a group of people on a similar journey to his own. This felt like such a massive step forward. Just like at the NRH, there was a real mix of people receiving treatment at STEPS. It wasn't long of course before Seán made some friends. This is a real constant in Seán's life; he was good at it before the attack, and he's still good at it now. Amy was in the room next door to Seán and before long they got to know one another. She was only in her twenties and was a teacher. She was also a wheelchair user. Seán still couldn't communicate very well but that didn't matter. Amy found a way. I'd arrive sometimes to find them having an arm wrestle or a thumb war, always smiling, always laughing. She spent a lot of her time trying to encourage Seán to say different words. She was bubbly and fun, and she didn't give up until Seán finally said 'Amy'. It was lovely to witness the bond between the two of them. Amy was also really kind to me. She knew I was living close by on my own and she always went out of her way to make me feel included. At nighttime the centre organised different themed nights which Amy always made sure I was invited to. I think she wanted me to feel like part of the gang, which I really appreciated. She was a special person.

I had settled well into my new life in Sheffield despite the very bumpy start. After the trauma of that plane journey from Dunboyne, myself and Jack had collected my luggage at STEPS, which had arrived by courier. We got a taxi and I gave the driver the address of the Airbnb I had been given. I was thrilled when the taxi pulled up outside the apartment 10 minutes later. It was very close by, which meant I could walk back and forth to Seán every day. The two-bedroom apartment was in an old Victorian house and it felt very homely. It was warm and cosy and the woman I was renting it from had left a bottle of wine and a little starter pack in the fridge, which was such a lovely thing to do. That night myself and Jack found a local pub to unwind from the day. Over a glass of wine and a pint we chatted about the horror of the plane journey and the fright we'd both had. I was tired but, overall, I had a sense of calm. We had made it to Sheffield. Seán was safe and in the best place for him, and I felt safe too. We were ready for our next adventure.

One Step at a Time

I knew that Seán wasn't going to leave STEPS walking and talking. I was aware of the severity of his brain injury, so I was constantly managing my expectations. But I also knew that many people with brain injuries make significant recovery gains with the help of prolonged intensive rehab. Part of the ethos at STEPS was recognising that each brain injury is unique and therefore the timescale of someone's recovery and how well they respond to different therapies can be different for everyone. I liked this approach and it was one of the things that drew me to this centre over any other. It helped me to stay hopeful. Maybe Seán would recover in ways no one expected him to. I had a lot of meetings with Seán's case manager in STEPS where we talked through different goals for Seán. Improving his mobility and his speech were the main two priorities. We knew Seán could hear us and understand a lot of what we were saying but verbally he was still very challenged.

He had shown an interest in music therapy while he was in the NRH so the therapists in STEPS began to engage him in 'melodic therapy'. This involved Seán working with a speech and language therapist and a music therapist in an attempt to put some words to music. The idea behind it is if a patient loses themselves in the melody of the music, words may just come out. This therapy took place in the music room in STEPS which housed a beautiful piano and other instruments. The therapists worked on some key phrases with Seán. Simple sentences like, 'I want to go to bed,' 'I want a cup of tea,' or 'I'm in pain.' We really wanted Seán to be able to articulate his needs. The progress was very gradual, but Seán persevered and eventually, in a whisper, some words came back. His voice was so much lower than it had been before the attack because the tracheostomy had been in place for so long. It was so strange to hear his voice again after not hearing it for so long. Seán also took part in another interesting therapy called 'voice skills'. A group of five or six people worked together for a session which also took place in the music room. On arriving into the room everyone was given either a recorder or a tin whistle, which they were encouraged to play. At the end of the session there was always a quiz, which was Seán's favourite part. The aim of the game was to guess what lyric was coming next. For instance, therapist would begin 'Somewhere over the …' then pause for a moment before Seán jumped in with 'Rainbow'. He was delighted with himself. We had been trying to get Seán to finish our sentences over the previous months and he had started to make some progress when prompted. On Seán's very last voice skills session at STEPS the other clients organised a special rendition of 'You'll Never Walk Alone'. It was so emotional and very, very special.

Seán's mobility also needed a lot of work. One of the goals we had set for him was to get him to be able to sit on the side of a bed safely. This was something that caused him huge difficulty. He had lost all control of his core so he would wobble from side to side, and if someone wasn't with him, he could possibly hurt himself. His physiotherapist worked hard on this and before long Seán mastered it. It was a massive achievement. Seán also used the hydrotherapy pool twice a week, which I was thrilled about as he had never had an opportunity to do that in Ireland.

The clients had their down days too. They all worked so hard and it was very tough for them. Every effort was made to try to prevent the inevitable monotony of being in any type of medical setting for a prolonged period. Management and staff believed that if the clients were entertained, they were more likely to stay engaged for longer. In addition to the themed nights that were held, staff also organised pampering treats for their clients and pet therapy, too. Jemima the duck was a very regular visitor. Somehow, the staff managed to always put a smile on people's faces.

On one of the days when I had first arrived in Sheffield, I got a text from my first cousin Terry. Her dad was my mam's brother. He was a prison officer who years before had emigrated to England where he met his wife and had his family. Terry now lived in Sheffield. We had lost touch over the years but out of the blue I got this text message. She had heard about what had happened to Seán and had contacted my sister Bernie who had told her I had now moved to Sheffield to be with Seán while he had his rehab at STEPS. She couldn't believe it. She got my details from Bernie and now we were arranging to meet for coffee. Having Terry in Sheffield gave me a sense of home and familiarity even though I hadn't seen her in years. She was so good to me. I didn't have a car so she brought me grocery shopping so I could do a big shop if I needed to. She worked as an occupational therapist, so she was hugely interested in Seán and how he was progressing. She even came to a lot of the meetings I had with the therapists at STEPS. We became close and my time in Sheffield was made much easier because of her.

I was also helped along this leg of the journey by the old reliables, the members of our 'Seán's Recovery' WhatsApp group. Just as they had when Seán was in The Walton Centre, in Beaumont Hospital and most recently at the NRH, they were on hand with whatever help I needed. Another rota was set up and the bed in my spare room became a rolling resting place for all those who wanted to support Seán. No bed ever had its sheets changed so often. As the weeks passed, Seán began to make significant progress. He was settled and happy. It was then that I began to consider something that had been in the back of my head for a while now: bringing Seán back to Anfield to watch his beloved Liverpool play on their home turf. As a family we had always said we'd get him back one day, but we didn't really know if it would be possible. I'm sure it seemed strange to people – it was after all the scene of the crime, the place where our worst nightmare had happened. But Seán's lifelong love of sport, particularly Liverpool and GAA, was still with him. And over the previous 18 months as Seán had become more alert and more engaged, we knew that love was still very much alive in his heart. At one stage it would have seemed like a pipe dream, a total impossibility. But as he improved, we began to give it some consideration. If it was ever going to happen, now was the time, when we were in Sheffield, as it wasn't too far to travel. Stephen Felle contacted Liverpool FC CEO Peter Moore and the plans were put in place for Seán to attend the top of the table clash between Liverpool and Manchester City at the beginning of November 2019. This was a positive step for Seán, something I knew he would get a huge boost from. I knew it was going to be bittersweet for me, Jack, Shauna and Emma but it was something we had to do.

An Emotional Return

It was a foggy November day when the taxi pulled up outside STEPS to take us to Anfield. Jack was visiting Seán in Sheffield at the time, so we travelled together. We were meeting Shauna and Emma, who were flying into Liverpool from Dublin. The return to Anfield, the place their dad had been attacked, was emotional for all three of them. Emma fell asleep on the flight which was packed with Liverpool fans heading for Anfield. She had a photograph of Seán on her phone and when she woke up, she felt the man sitting the other side of her knew who she was. She couldn't wait to get off the flight. Emma inherited my shyness. Seán used to slag her that if we were all starving Emma wouldn't ring for a takeaway. It was a running joke in our house. The fact that Seán's story had become a very public one weighed heavily on all three of them at times. It wasn't something any of them wanted but they all knew we had to fundraise if their dad was going to be able to access the rehab he needed and deserved.

Over the previous days I had started to prepare Seán for what was happening. I knew that this was the most important game of the season. Liverpool were going into the game as league leaders. They were five points ahead of Man City and the game was billed as the ultimate 'six pointer'. Man City had pipped Liverpool to the title by just one point the previous season, so every point was crucial. It was going to be a tense and exciting game. If Liverpool won, it would put them eight points ahead of their rivals, but a City win would close the gap to just two points. I told Seán all about our plans to go to Anfield. 'This is for you, Seán, you're Liverpool's guest of honour,' I told him. STEPS offered a member of staff to accompany us to make sure Seán was comfortable, which of course led to great competition for the slot in the days before the match. Liverpool FC had done all they could do to make sure the visit went as smoothly as possible and that Seán was as comfortable as he could be. Myself, Jack, Seán and his occupational therapist made our way into the taxi. The journey should have taken less than two hours, but the foggy conditions made it much longer. I remember sitting in the back of the taxi looking out at the foggy moors. I didn't really know how Seán was going to react to being back in Anfield. I have never really talked to him about the attack. He knows he was injured and that his brain doesn't work in the same way now, but I've always been determined to keep things positive for him, to focus on the future and not the past.

Eventually we pulled up to a designated area right outside the stadium. I looked at Seán and he had this massive smile on his face. I knew I had nothing to worry about – he knew exactly where he was, and he couldn't have been happier. As we got him out of the taxi and started to make our way into the grounds, I could hear some people saying, 'Look, that's Seán Cox.' It was surreal. We were whisked into a lift and straight to the Director's Box. As soon as the doors opened, we were greeted and shown to our table. The room was full of dinner tables laid with the best linen and silver. As soon as we took our seats Liverpool FC CEO Peter Moore and Kenny Dalglish came over to say hello to Seán. I remembered back to the time King Kenny had come to see me when Seán was in The Walton Centre. I shuddered at the memory of how gravely ill Seán was back then. Yes, he still had a mountain to climb but he really had come a long way. The girl who was serving our table also made a beeline for Seán. Her cousin had been one of the nurses who had cared for Seán in the ICU at The Walton Centre. She had heard he was coming to the match and had been hoping to meet him. Her cousin had often talked about him after he left Liverpool to come back to Dublin. We took photos of her and Seán so she could show her cousin how far he had come.

Before long it was time for us to take our seats for the buildup to the match. The atmosphere was electric and the whole stadium was buzzing. Two seats had been cut out of the stand in the Director's Box for Seán's wheelchair to fit in. The night was cold, but the atmosphere was warm and welcoming. We were getting the full VIP treatment, including little blankets to put over our laps and an endless supply of tea and hot chocolate. The view from our seats was incredible. Since I had started planning this trip weeks beforehand, I had been worried that I wouldn't enjoy it – not because I'm not a big football fan but because I'd feel too sad. Yes, it was true that it was great that Seán was well enough to return to Anfield, but he wasn't the same Seán as before the attack. He wasn't sitting in the Kop with his brothers or his friends the way he had hundreds of times before. This was different. He was in a wheelchair. He couldn't walk. His injuries were life-changing. We had such a long road ahead of us. As I was lost in my thoughts those familiar lyrics started to fill the air. 'When you walk through a storm, hold your head up high and don't be afraid of the dark, at the end of a storm, there's a golden sky and the sweet silver song of the lark.' I looked across at Seán who was sitting there with the biggest smile on his face. His arms were in the air as he belted out 'You'll Never Walk Alone'. How could I not be happy? Before the match Liverpool manager Jürgen Klopp has said the attack on Seán was 'the lowest point of his time at Liverpool' and that Seán's return to the stadium would be 'one of his highlights'. In the matchday programme, Klopp wrote, 'Seán's name and that of his wife Martina and his family makes me think of courage, spirit and renewal, Seán is an inspirational figure in this club's story now.'

The Reds got off to a flying start and were two up inside the first 15 minutes with goals from Fabinho and Salah. The second half saw Sadio Mané's header make it 3–0. City pulled one back, but it was Liverpool's night. The win put them eight points clear at the top of the Premier League. The stadium erupted. It was massive for the club. I think it was at this point that the club really started to believe this was finally their year. Afterwards Peter Moore brought us down to the tunnel just outside the media centre. The players and members of the media mingled together as post-match interviews were carried out. Some of Seán's footballing heroes like Mo Salah, Jordan Henderson, Trent Alexander-Arnold, Joe Gomez and Virgil van Dijk came to say hello. Seán was completely star-struck. He recognised all of them, and as they shook his hand, he pulled them in for a hug. I knew the trip to Anfield would give Seán a boost but I never in my wildest dreams thought he'd lap it up like this. They were all so generous with their time that evening; it was lovely to see. When I later saw some of the photographs that had been taken, I couldn't get over Seán's smile. It spoke a thousand words.

Just as we were about to make our way back up to the VIP area a door opened and out came Jürgen Klopp. What happened next is very hard to describe. They both just looked at one another and started to embrace. Neither of them wanted to let go. It was a real genuine moment. In his post-match press conference, Klopp told the assembled media, 'Yes, I met Seán, it was very nice, he was very happy to see me and I thought I'm much more happy to see him. I think we had a draw.' We had been through a lot of big moments with Seán at this stage, but I knew this was going to be the standout one. It was special, and not because of where we were, or the special treatment, or the footballing stars. It was because Seán was so happy. He had enjoyed the Liverpool Vs Ireland Legends match at the Aviva Stadium seven months earlier, but he had come on a lot since then. I thought back to how tired he'd become at the Aviva and how at one stage I had to bring him to the back of the room to have a rest. It was hard to see him like that. As a family we had also enjoyed the gala night at the Intercontinental Hotel, but I wasn't the only one who really missed Seán that night. I realised afterwards that we'd all been feeling the same way. As heartwarming as it was to see the support and goodwill for Seán in that room that night, it was so hard to know he was lying in a hospital bed less than 10 kilometres away. We had been celebrating him, without him. This was different. Seán was happy and alert. He didn't tire once. We were in Anfield as a family and I know that day will stay with us forever.

Baby STEPS

As 2019 came to an end, so did our time in Sheffield. Seán had undergone 14 weeks of intensive therapy at STEPS Rehabilitation. It was now time to go home. His three-month stay was a drop in the ocean compared to most of the other clients, many of whom were able to fund their rehab through large insurance claims. We were funding this privately, something we would never have been able to do if it wasn't for all those who helped us to fundraise for Seán's care. I was leaving Sheffield with the same mix of emotions I had arrived with. I couldn't wait to get Seán back to our family home in Dunboyne, but I was also anxious that he would regress without the constant and varied schedule of therapy he had been lucky enough to complete. He had come on hugely over that three-month period. I couldn't help but wonder what progress he'd make if we could stay for longer. But the world-class therapy that's on offer in STEPS comes at a substantial cost so, for now, we had to say goodbye.

The house was still being renovated and wasn't going to be ready for another few months so I asked the McNultys if

Seán could return to Marymount Care Centre in Lucan until we had everything ready for him. Seán had spent eight weeks there when he left the National Rehabilitation Hospital in Dún Laoghaire before we had come to STEPS and it had been such a positive experience for him. Caring for someone with a brain injury was not a regular occurrence at Marymount, so some of the team had attended his discharge meeting from the NRH. It was a bit of a learning curve for them all, but they really threw themselves into it. When he arrived, he was welcomed with open arms. He couldn't believe his luck with his own private room that had a TV and a big window that looked out into the garden. All the nurses and carers were so kind to him and they made a huge effort to get to know him and his ways of communicating. I was so relieved that there was a bed there for him on our return to Ireland until his own bed was ready for him at home. As we began our last week in Sheffield, I reflected a lot on how far we had come. Both of us. I had learned so much during Seán's stay at Sheffield, about what was ahead of us when we did eventually get back to our own house. My aim from the very beginning was to get Seán back to where he belonged. It's hard to even express how much I missed his presence. Seán had left that morning to go to a match and had never came home. In a way it felt like he disappeared overnight. I longed for the most run-of-the-mill ordinary things like him being there when I woke up in the morning or him coming in from work in the evening time. His seat at our kitchen table was empty. I wasn't the only one – all four of us couldn't wait to have him back where he belonged. The five of us had spent so many evenings chatting over dinner, catching up on what had happened that day for each of us, making our plans, laughing and of course arguing too. We wanted all of that back. I was also aware that I wasn't qualified to properly care for someone with a brain injury. I had a lot to learn. When we'd arrived at STEPS, I had decided this was where I was going to do just that.

Living in Sheffield allowed me to attend most of Seán's therapies with him to get a sense of how it all worked. I watched the therapists closely as they used their well-honed skills to coax him along even on days when he was tired and fed up. I admired the patience they had when progress was slow and the encouraging words they used when Seán made some headway. They built up such a rapport with him and even on the bad days their outlook remained positive. I took note of everything and asked as many questions as I could. STEPS was using the best therapies and practices, they were the experts, so I soaked up every bit of knowledge I could. I hoped that Seán would return to STEPS in the future, but while he was at home, I knew it was important to keep up the work in the meantime. If I watched and listened and learned, I could take some of the magic from STEPS back home to Dunboyne. It wasn't just the world-class therapies we were going to miss. It was also very hard to say goodbye to all the people who had worked with Seán and all the friends he had met along the way. When you spend all day, every day in a centre like STEPS you develop a bond with the other people there. Each one is on their own journey with their own story. There was a different reason why each person ended up in STEPS, but they had a common goal: to get better, whatever better was for them.

One of the big goals we had set for Seán at the beginning was to get him to take a few steps with a walker, aided by two people. He had only ever done this before with the help of three people but the team at STEPS felt Seán had gained enough strength to do it with just two. Seán could move his right leg but not his left. The physiotherapists put so much effort into preparing Seán to achieve this goal. He was determined to do it himself too and worked so hard with the team, doing everything that was asked of him. Then two days before we left Sheffield to come home his team of physios said, 'Right, Seán. Let's do this today.' They got him set up and talked him through what was going to happen, reminding him of all the tips and advice they'd given him before. I stood there holding my breath, and then he did it. The therapists were helping his left leg along, but it was still significant progress. I burst into tears at the sight of him moving one foot in front of the other. When I looked around I realised everyone else was emotional too. They were so invested in his progress, it felt like it meant as much to them as it did to me. Seeing Seán standing upright with just two people by his side was such an achievement. I had forgotten how tall he is. I had become so used to seeing him lying down or in his wheelchair, it was incredible to see this tall man standing beside me. He was so proud of himself; he knew how far he'd come. We were leaving STEPS very much on a high note. But first we had to say our goodbyes.

Amy, Seán's friend in the room beside him, was sad to see us go. She made such a fuss of him during his last week. As well as being such a bubbly, optimistic young woman, she was also an incredible artist. She made Seán a gorgeous handmade card with 'You'll Never Walk Alone' written on the front of it. She got all the staff members and other clients to sign it and on the last night we all had dinner together and they presented it to Seán. 'You'll come back now, won't you, Seán?' they asked, as we enjoyed our last supper together. I had already made a promise to Seán that I'd do everything I could to get him back to STEPS as often as I could afford over the next few years. The difference it had made to him was too great to ignore. The following morning, we got our final bits organised and said our last goodbyes. We were leaving Sheffield the same way we had arrived, in the tiny private plane, but this time we were better prepared. I made sure Seán had very little to eat for his breakfast and I had bought anti-sickness medicine to give to him before the flight. Nonetheless I was nervous, and praying for a smoother journey than we'd experienced on the way over. It was quite emotional when we saw the pilot because he couldn't believe the difference in Seán – he saw a massive improvement in him.

A short time later we landed in Dunboyne safely with no scary incidents to report. Before we brought Seán to Marymount Care Centre we drove by our house. I had talked to Seán a lot about going home from STEPS, but it was hard to explain that he wasn't going 'home home' just yet. I had shown him pictures of the work that was being carried out, the scaffolding outside the house, a digger sitting in what used to be our living room, the walls that had been knocked down, but I wanted him to see it properly. I wanted him to know it wouldn't be too much longer until he was back there with us. A few weeks later we celebrated Christmas of

2019 in my sister Catherine's house in Knocklyon. Around 20 of us sat down to the most beautiful meal with Seán at the head of the table. It was a far cry from the previous year. And I knew by the time Christmas 2020 rolled around we'd be 'home home'. Before we said goodbye to 2019 Seán also achieved another major milestone. He returned to St Peter's GAA Club in Dunboyne for the first time since the attack. Fergus McNulty really wanted to get him back, so he suggested we make a visit to watch Liverpool play Wolves in the Premier League on 29 December. Fergus arranged everything and made sure all of Seán's close friends were there to welcome him back. The place erupted when we wheeled Seán in. Liverpool won the match and Seán was thrilled to see everyone. One of Jack's friends was working behind the bar and Seán kept waving his hand for a pint. He thoroughly enjoyed a proper pint of Guinness surrounded by his nearest and dearest. It was the perfect end to a year of so many ups and downs.

NOW

2020

As 2020 dawned, I wrote a list of New Year's resolutions. I had no idea how many of them I'd achieve over the next 12 months, but I wrote them down anyway. There was one I was definitely going to tick off the list, and that was getting Seán back where he belonged, in our home in Dunboyne. This had been my goal all along. I knew if I fought hard enough I'd make it happen, some day. It was what we all wanted. The attack on Seán had robbed us of almost two years of living like a normal family, under one roof. Something we took for granted. The five of us being reunited at home was now in touching distance. I also wanted, and needed, to return to work. Management at Dunnes Stores had been so supportive since Seán had been attacked. I had really enjoyed being back in work when Seán was in the NRH. It had given me back a little bit of my old life. It's such a busy environment that it always took my mind off what had happened and in a way stopped me worrying too much about what the future might bring. I had to leave again when we decided to move to Sheffield for Seán to start his rehab at STEPS. I was hopeful that with the right care plan in place for Seán at home I'd return again. I also hoped that 2020 would see Seán return to Sheffield for another stint of rehab. A 12-week stay comes at a massive cost but I just couldn't ignore the progress he had made during his time there. He had come such a long way in such a short space of time. He left STEPS doing things we never thought he'd be able to do. Without the generosity people had shown us we would never have been able to do this. Where would Seán be now if we hadn't been in a position to access rehab in the UK? It wasn't worth thinking about. When we said goodbye to everyone at STEPS in December I knew we'd be going back.

I also really wanted us to take a trip back to The Walton Centre in Liverpool to retrieve Seán's patient diary. We had all spent so much time filling it out during those long early days when Seán was still so ill. My approach to Seán's journey has always been to keep looking forward instead of back, but I knew if I revisited that time it would highlight to me just how far Seán had come. I knew I'd have to dig deep to go back there. The memory of the shock and terror I had felt on that very first morning when myself and Peter pulled up outside the hospital still made my blood run cold. But it was where Seán's life was saved. I really don't know if he would have survived if the doctors at The Walton Centre hadn't looked after him so well. It was also where he opened his eyes for the very first time, giving us the hope we so badly needed that he wasn't gone. As hard as it would be to go back, I knew it would be a positive step for Seán.

Then there was Portugal. Our trip to Lagos to find our home away from home now seemed like something that had happened to someone else in a different life. I thought back on the day we had viewed the apartment and how we both knew it was 'the one'. That night we had planned to talk it through over dinner but before long we were celebrating. We had already started to imagine all the good times we'd have there in the future with Jack, Shauna and Emma and our families and friends. As Seán fought for his life in intensive care we should have been in Lagos closing the sale on the apartment. That certainly wasn't going to happen now. But what about a holiday? Would that be possible? I wasn't sure. But as we entered 2020 I had a real desire to bring Seán back to Portugal, for the five of us to have a family holiday. We had so many happy memories of all the summers we had spent there, it was truly a special place for us as a family. Logistically I knew it would be really difficult. We'd have to navigate the airport and the flight and then there was Seán's personal care, like showering and moving him from a bed to a chair. I wasn't sure if it would work but if the past two years had taught me anything it was that nothing is impossible, so I promised myself I'd look into it.

This was going to be the year we got some sense of our old lives back. The past 18 months had been so difficult for Seán and for us as a family. We had been on such a journey since Seán had been attacked, one that had taken us from The Walton Centre in Liverpool to Beaumont Hospital, from there to the National Rehabilitation Hospital and then to STEPS in Sheffield. Seán was now happy in Marymount Care Centre in Lucan until he made his final journey home to Dunboyne. It had been a time of such immense worry and anxiety. I had to come to terms with what had happened to Seán. I then had to get my head around his injury and how it was going to change our lives forever. I had to process the fact that the old Seán was gone, and that things were very different now. And then I had to accept that I was in charge. This was such an adjustment for me. Myself and Seán had always worked well as a team, we made decisions together, we consulted one another, we encouraged one another, we picked each other up when the other one was down. We had been together for more than 30 years; readjusting to this new reality was hard. Navigating this road for both of us felt like a massive responsibility. It was a lonelier path than I'd been used to. I had to make the right choices about Seán's care, I needed to get the house ready for his return, and I wanted to be there for Jack, Shauna and Emma.

Even the smallest jobs and decisions were more difficult now. A few months after Seán had been attacked, my mobile phone started to act up. I ignored it for ages but eventually it gave up on me. I went into a phone shop to see what option I had to upgrade it or get a new phone. Seán had bought me the phone so the account was in his name. I explained everything to the girl in the shop. I told her my husband had bought the phone but he had been injured and now had a serious brain injury. I needed to transfer the account into my own name. 'Well, unless he walks in here and tells me that himself, there's nothing I can do for you,' she replied over the counter of the busy phone shop. I was gobsmacked. I turned on my heel and walked out, tears rolling down my face before I even made it to the door. This journey we were on was far from straightforward but I knew I had to do everything I could to make the best of a really bad situation.

I had cried way too many tears. We all had. But as we entered the second week of the new year that was about to change.

A few months before this the chairman of the Seán Cox Rehabilitation Trust, Stephen Felle, had been driving home from Dublin Airport one evening when his mobile rang. It was an English number and when he answered a man called John said 'Hello' in a Liverpool accent. He explained to Stephen that he wanted to come to Dublin to do something for Seán Cox and that he had been told to ring this number. Stephen was just about to enter the Port Tunnel so knowing he'd lose his signal he told John he'd call him back. A short time later Stephen received a work call and it slipped his mind. There was still a lot of public interest in Seán's story. What had happened to him really seemed to hit a nerve with people and Stephen often got calls from different organisations wanting to fundraise for the 'Support Seán' initiative. A few hours later Stephen's phone rang again. John from Liverpool was ringing back. Stephen apologised for forgetting to get back to him and asked him to send an email with the details of the event he was proposing. 'But Peter Moore told me I needed to talk to you,' said John. Surprised to hear his mobile number had been passed on by the CEO of Liverpool FC, Stephen asked the man his name again. 'John Bishop' came the reply. It was the very famous Liverpudlian comedian and avid Liverpool supporter. Stephen was mortified the penny hadn't dropped sooner and apologised for not recognising his voice. John Bishop went on to explain that he really wanted to organise a fundraising night for Seán. He was proposing a gig in Dublin in January of 2020 and was ringing Stephen to ask would it be okay with Seán's family. 'Where are you thinking?' enquired Stephen. 'The 3Arena,' said John. 'I don't need you to do anything, maybe just help with the publicity of it, but I'll take care of the rest.' And that is how we found ourselves making our way from Dunboyne into Dublin city centre on a cold Friday night in January for a night of laughter hosted by some of Ireland and Britain's top comedians.

Myself and Seán travelled together along with Jack, Shauna, Emma and Jack's girlfriend, Laura. One of Seán's carers from Marymount Care Centre, Joan, also came with us to help me with Seán. We pulled up outside the 3Arena and were brought in through a side entrance. A room had been set up for us in case Seán needed to rest at any stage during the night. We went in and got Seán settled. John Bishop came in to say hello to us and we thanked him for all he had done to organise the night. We had met him before at a match and he had always been so supportive. Like many people, John felt what happened to Seán could have happened to anyone. He said Seán was just like any other football fan on his way to watch his team playing a big game when the unthinkable happened. He wanted to help us so he called in the help of his friends. More than 8,000 people bought tickets for the star-studded line-up he had managed to pull together. He was going to be joined on stage by Michael McIntyre, Dara Ó Briain, Deirdre O'Kane, Des Bishop, Jason Byrne, Joanne McNally and Tommy Tiernan. They had all jumped at the chance to be part of the night. Before long they began to arrive at the 3Arena and came in to say hello to Seán. He recognised all of them. He loved comedy, live shows or comedy on the TV. He always had a great sense of humour and he loved a good laugh. Jason Byrne was so natural with Seán. He really knew how to communicate with him. He kept pointing to nice things in the room and telling Seán to hide them in his jacket and bring them home. Seán thought he was hilarious. We were taken to our seats as the gig was about to get underway. The night before, Stephen Felle had met John Bishop for a drink to thank him for pulling the show together. They got chatting about how much Seán loved Liverpool and in particular Jürgen Klopp. John picked up his phone and asked Jürgen to record a video message for Seán to be played at the start of the gig. He agreed. As we took our seats Jürgen's face filled the big screen. 'Hello and good evening from Liverpool to Dublin,' he began as the crowd erupted in applause. He went on to say meeting Seán at Anfield had been one of his best moments as a Liverpool supporter. 'Seán Cox is a special guy with a special family and I could see in his eyes he was full of love for this football club. Seán Cox feels part of our family and we feel part of the Seán Cox family,' he said. He finished by introducing the man responsible for the night, 'the one and only John Bishop'.

Each comedian took to the stage. I hadn't seen Seán laugh this much since the attack. I had to fight back the tears as I watched his face light up beside me. Near the end of the gig he started to get tired. I decided to bring him back to the room for a little rest. Just as I was about to get him organised to leave our seats, John Bishop announced they had something special planned for Seán. I sat back down. All eight comedians arrived out onto the stage as that familiar music began to fill the arena. The comedians led the crowd of 8,000 in a rendition of 'You'll Never Walk Alone' that I thought was going to take the roof off the 3Arena. Everyone had their arms in the air waving them from side to side, shining the lights on their phones. Seán was so moved. We all were. It was an extremely emotional and special night. It gave Seán such a boost for the last bit of his journey before we'd have him home. I was so grateful to John and all of the comedians who took part, also to Aiken Promotions and the 3Arena. Afterwards John Bishop said, 'Sometimes in life something wonderful comes out of something tragic,' and he was right. As we made our way home that night I made a vow to laugh more in 2020. It certainly is the best medicine.

The gig raised €465,000 for the Seán Cox Rehabilitation Trust. It brought the total amount of money raised over the previous 18 months for Seán's care to €2.7 million euro. I almost couldn't get my head around the generosity we had been shown. I was so grateful to every single person who had played their part in making an awful situation so much better than it might have been for Seán and for us as a family. People donating their hard-earned cash was something I never took for granted and from the very beginning I was determined the money would be used carefully to make sure Seán had the care and support he deserved. I knew Seán's long-term care was going to exceed what we had raised but I also knew it was time to wind down our fundraising efforts. There are so many other charities and causes across Ireland and the UK that need public support too. So many people had taken Seán and us into their hearts. I really hoped other families going through difficult times would also get to experience the same goodwill we had.

Timing Is Everything

My plans to get Seán home to our house were progressing well. I don't know how, but through everything that had happened over the previous 20 months I had always managed to hold on to a little bit of hope in my heart that this would happen someday. Even in the very early days as I sat by Seán's bedside holding his hand in the ICU of The Walton Centre in Liverpool, not knowing if he would even survive, I told myself that eventually we'd come home together. I thought back on how we had ended up buying our house in Dunboyne all those years ago and how we had promised each other this was our last house move. This was our forever home and I wasn't going to live there without Seán. The house renovations were coming along well. There was a lot to be done to make sure Seán would be comfortable and safe at home. Everything needed to be remodelled.

The house was almost 20 years old so all the floors had to be levelled off to ensure that Seán would be safe in his wheelchair. We removed all the walls and made downstairs mostly open plan. Seán is still in a manual wheelchair and we don't know if he will ever progress to an electric one. His peripheral vision was damaged in the attack so it may not be suitable, but if it did happen in the future, I wanted to make sure he'd be able to move around freely downstairs. We reversed the layout, moving our kitchen to the front of the house. Our old kitchen is now Seán's bedroom, which looks out onto the back garden. We also put a bathroom with a shower off his bedroom. When we were planning the renovations, I really wanted Seán to have a separate room for his therapies. When Seán had been in STEPS, I had seen the benefits of someone undergoing therapy having a space for sleep and relaxation and a separate space for work. I'm not sure people realise how hard work therapy is for the person who is doing it. I wanted Seán to be able to distinguish places in the house that were for him to just live in and then he could go to his dedicated therapy room when it was time for 'work'. A separate room at the back where Seán could do all his physiotherapy would also give us some extra space for his considerable amount of equipment. Seán has two wheelchairs: one for every day and a smaller one for when we go out in the car. We'd also need his standing turner, with splints to support his legs, to move Seán from his bed to his recliner chair and his shower chair. The builder was a big Liverpool supporter and he was pulling out all the stops, doing everything he could to get things ready for Seán.

We'd also been shown such goodwill from different suppliers who were familiar with Seán's story and wanted to do something to help. Good progress was being made and we knew we'd be able to move back in by the middle of February. We decided that myself, Jack, Shauna and Emma would move back first to make sure everything was in order. We'd then bring Seán back. We were so excited at the thought of having him under the same roof as us again. We had done so much trekking around the place between different hospitals but now we'd be properly reunited as a family. It was never going to be possible for Seán to come home without the help of carers. We had been assigned a case manager who worked for the Health Service Executive and Acquired Brain Injury Ireland. Over the previous months she had assessed Seán in order to make a recommendation about his care needs. She had travelled to visit Seán in STEPS in Sheffield twice to determine what supports and services Seán would need access to in order to live his life at home as comfortably as possible. She completed her assessment and submitted her recommendation for sign-off. Once the builders gave us the green light to move back in by mid-February, I contacted our case manager. I had been warned by a few people with experience in this area that I might have to hound the HSE to make sure the services would be there for Seán when he needed to use them. After a couple of unanswered calls, I started to get worried. Everyone knew our plan was to bring Seán home and everyone knew that would be impossible without a care package in place. Seán's needs were very high. Surely we weren't going to fall at the last hurdle?

Then on 24 January 2020 I received a call from the HSE. It was our case manager's boss. Finally, I was getting to talk to the person who had the power to green-light Seán's return home. But within seconds my hopes were dashed. 'I don't know how to say this to you, Martina,' she began. 'There is no funding in Meath, no care hours are available, we can't offer Seán anything.' My head started to spin. 'What do you mean?' I asked her. 'This makes no sense at all. You've had someone working on Seán's case for almost a year, she has been to visit him in the UK twice, she has seen how much care he needs, and now you're telling me there is nothing on offer?' She apologised and said the only thing she could do was make the request for funding at a national level. She promised she'd come back to me. A week later she called me back. The minute she said hello I knew by the tone of her voice it was more bad news. 'You're not going to like this, Martina,' she began. The request had gone to national level and there was no funding available. 'What do I do?' I asked her. 'I can't bring Seán home without a care plan in place – it's not possible.'

'I'm sorry,' she replied. 'I really don't know what to say to you.' I was so livid. I just couldn't believe what I was hearing. Our lives had been turned upside-down, but we had come this far. With all of us backing him Seán had battled to get to this point. The next step was to get him home. I would not let the rug be pulled from underneath us. Seán was happy in Marymount Care Centre but he wasn't staying there indefinitely. That was not a long-term plan. I wasn't going to take this sitting down. I was too angry. I had to break the news to the children and to Seán's family. It wasn't just me who was looking forward to getting Seán home – everyone was. This was a massive milestone and something we had all been working towards for nearly two years now. We had all played our part; we were all in this together. That evening I decided to let Fergus McNulty and Stephen Felle know what had happened. Maybe they'd know what to do. Fergus had a lot of dealings with the HSE through his work with Marymount Care Centre. Maybe he'd know who to call or what our next step should be. But I just couldn't bring myself to talk to them yet. I was still so angry, but the sadness had descended now too. We had been led to believe that Seán was entitled to care, which meant a life at home in his own house with his family was a possibility. And now we'd hit a roadblock. I was just so upset by the whole thing I couldn't even talk. Jack made the phone calls and explained the latest development. No one could understand how we had come this far for the process to stop like this. We decided to write to the health minister, Simon Harris. A letter and an email were sent outlining our concerns. All I could do was wait. It was one week before the general election 2020.

Polling was to take place the following Saturday, 8 February, the first time in decades that a vote had been held on a Saturday. We were still living in our rented accommodation in Dunboyne as we waited to move back into our house. That Saturday morning, one week before the vote, there was a knock on the door and Jack answered it. I was pottering around the kitchen when he arrived back in. 'Who was that?' I said to him. 'Not sure,' he said, 'some man canvassing for Fine Gael.' Well, I thought to myself, this is my chance. Wearing pyjama bottoms and a pair of socks, I took off out the door, leaving Jack behind. I must have looked like a lunatic as I made my way around the housing estate in search of the canvassers. Eventually I met a local Fine Gael Councillor from our area called Maria Murphy. She was also out canvassing for our local TD Regina Doherty, the Minister for Social Protection and Employment Affairs. 'I need to see

Regina,' I said to her. 'I need to talk to her.' In fairness to Maria Murphy, she asked Regina Doherty to come up to the house and we gathered in the sitting room. I told her exactly what had happened with Seán's care package. 'We're just about to bring him home,' I explained to her. 'I know he's disabled and has a long road ahead of him,' I continued, 'but we want to walk that road with him. He's a young man in a nursing home and I want to bring him back to where he belongs, in our house with me and his children. That's impossible without a care package.' Regina Doherty listened and took notes and we said our goodbyes. I'm not sure if it was our letter to Simon Harris, my chance meeting with Regina Doherty on the front doorstep, similar appeals I had made to our local Fianna Fáil TD Helen McEntee about the unfairness of what was happening to Seán, or a combination of everything, but someone somewhere had listened. A week later my mobile rang. It was our case manager. Seán's care package had been approved. I was going to get the help of a care team in the morning time for a few hours to help me with Seán and then again in the evening. It meant Seán could come home.

They say timing is everything, and in this case it certainly was. A date was agreed: 25 March 2020. The day we would bring Seán back to our forever home. It would be almost two years since Seán had taken his little overnight bag, kissed me on the head and headed for Dublin Airport to get his early morning flight to Liverpool. I felt like the day could not come quickly enough so I kept myself busy making sure everything was in order for Seán. A company called Comfort Keepers had been chosen by the HSE to provide

Seán with the care he needed. The carers who were going to be helping me to look after Seán began to get to know him at Marymount Care Centre. I also set about organising a schedule of therapy for Seán to do at home. I wanted him to have a full schedule of therapy to give him the best chance of recovery possible. He needed intensive speech and language therapy and physio. He had always enjoyed and responded well to music therapy, so I wanted to continue that too. 'Seán needs as much rehab and stimulation as he can manage,' Professor Eldridge had warned me as we left The Walton Centre for Dublin. He had saved Seán's life and I was going to follow his advice. Eventually, everything was in order. On good days I felt like we had reached the finish line. But I knew Seán's journey was a marathon and in reality it was far from over. Getting him home was nonetheless a massive milestone. But then something else happened, and not just to us, but to the whole world.

COVID-19

My sister Catherine is the first person who ever mentioned the word 'coronavirus' to me. It was in January 2020 during a phone conversation. Her son Andrew's girlfriend is a Chinese girl called Lou, who had lived in Ireland for several years. The pair had decided to travel to her home in Shenyang in China to visit her parents. It was to be a trip of a lifetime. Lou would get to introduce Andrew to her mam and dad while also showing him around the tourist spots of her home city. On 21 January they headed off, full of excitement, but their dream holiday quickly turned into a nightmare when a lockdown was imposed to contain the spread of a deadly new virus called COVID-19. I felt so sorry for them that their trip had been ruined. They found it really hard to get home but after a lot of back and forth and rearranging everything they managed to fly back to Dublin on the last plane out of Shenyang before all flights in and out were grounded. As Catherine filled me in on how their trip had been disrupted, little did I think that this virus, that no one had ever heard of, was going to change the world over the next few months.

Before long the virus spread internationally and by the end of February the first case had been detected in Ireland. One evening as I arrived at Marymount Care Centre to visit Seán, I was informed that visiting was going to be restricted at the nursing home to keep the residents safe. At this stage we were starting to get a better picture of the virus and the message was clear: the elderly and vulnerable were the groups most at risk. I was told only two people could visit Seán, a decision I totally understood. Marymount wanted to do everything they could to make sure all their residents and staff were kept safe and COVID-free. But I knew this was going to be hard on Seán. Being stimulated by visits from his family and friends was what kept Seán going – it was a massive part of his recovery. He hadn't been home in almost two years: that's a lot of time to spend in a hospital setting. He was also so used to seeing Jack, Shauna and Emma and his brothers, sisters and friends regularly. I told myself he'd be home soon, that we'd manage. Then on 11 March it was announced that COVID-19 had claimed its first death in the Republic of Ireland, an elderly woman who had passed away at Naas General Hospital in Kildare. On the same day the World Health Organisation officially declared the global outbreak to be a pandemic. By the time St Patrick's Day rolled around everyone in Ireland was at home getting ready to watch the then Taoiseach Leo Varadkar address the nation. 'This is the calm before the storm – before the surge, and when it comes, and it will come, never will so many ask so much of so few,' he warned. This was a national holiday like no other, one that would certainly stay with people forever. Everything was cancelled, there were no parades or parties, no drowning of the shamrock. Instead everyone was at home.

At this stage the number of confirmed COVID-19 cases was still relatively small in Ireland, but this was soon to change. The people of Ireland were asked to 'come together by staying apart'. We were told the disease would be mild for many but older people and those with chronic diseases were at real risk. 'Many people will be hospitalised and sadly some people will die,' Leo Varadkar warned. It was obvious what was coming. I got into my car and made my way to Marymount Care Centre. The nursing home was going into lockdown. Only staff would be allowed through the doors in the hope of keeping the virus out. I panicked. I knew I had to get Seán out, I had to get him home, before it was too late. All eventualities started to run through my head. I knew it wasn't possible to just bring Seán home at that moment. I wanted to wheel him out to my car, put him in and drive him back to the safety of our house. But his needs were too substantial; we would never manage on our own. But I also couldn't leave him in the nursing home. What if he got the virus? Being on a ventilator in the ICU of The Walton Centre in Liverpool had left Seán's lungs compromised. He wasn't the strong, healthy man he had been before the attack. Would he be particularly vulnerable? I knew I could never live with myself if something happened. I felt so hopeless. After everything we had been through, and now this. Hadn't Seán battled enough, hadn't all of us? What if the lockdown lasted for weeks?

Leo Varadkar said no one knew when the virus would be under control and he warned it could go on for months into the summer. Seán contracting COVID-19 was unthinkable, but so was not being able to see him. I couldn't bear the thought of not being in constant contact with him. 'Technology can help – check in with your loved ones on Skype or Facetime and promise you'll see them again soon,' advised the Taoiseach. Seán's communication had improved but he was largely nonverbal. You couldn't hand Seán a phone and expect him to be able to speak into it. I was also worried about his mental health. He was so used to having so many visitors. Each one of them played a massive role in making sure Seán remained engaged in what was going on around him. I knew he'd be well looked after by the management and staff in Marymount – they had always been so good to him – but what would it do to him to be in there with no friends or family? He wouldn't understand what was going on. It would be impossible to explain it to him and I couldn't bear the thought of him wondering where his crew had disappeared to. Staying apart from Seán was just not an option. I had to get him home and I had to do it now.

A Happy Goodbye

Forty-eight hours later I wheeled Seán up our new path and through the front door of our home in Dunboyne. I had called Seán's case manager and told her we had to get Seán out of Marymount Care Centre before a full lockdown was implemented. I asked her to expedite the plans we had put in place for the end of the month. She agreed and put the wheels in motion. Jack and I drove to Marymount to collect Seán on 20 March 2020 armed with thank-you cards and a box of Krispy Kreme doughnuts. It was all I had time to organise. We just couldn't believe it was happening. Seán's brother Peter offered to use his van to transport Seán's equipment and belongings back to the house – his second wheelchair, the standing turner and his shower chair. Jack couldn't come into the nursing home because of the visiting restrictions so he waited outside. I walked in and made my way to Seán's room as I had done so many times before. There he was sitting in his wheelchair ready to come home. The room was empty, all his bits and pieces packed away. We made our way to the reception area where all the staff had gathered to say goodbye.

I had been so distracted by the panic of trying to get Seán home quicker than we had planned that I hadn't predicted how emotional it would be. It was only then, as I stood there in reception, did it hit me that this was an unusual situation for the people who worked in Marymount. Normally people don't leave a nursing home to go home. It's usually the place people spend their final years and their final days. This was different: they had minded Seán when he needed it, they had done all they could for him, and now it was time for him to go home. All the staff at Marymount had seen a change in him after his rehab at STEPS. Seán was only in his early fifties and what he lacked in communication skills he made up for with his sense of humour. As a result, he had managed to develop a wonderful relationship with a lot of the people who were looking after him in Marymount. He was incredibly fond of them and the feeling, I think, was mutual. He was really going to miss them. For a long time after Seán had regained consciousness and seemed alert, he didn't show many emotions. Now here he was sitting in his wheelchair in the reception of Marymount Care Centre with tears running down his face at the idea of saying goodbye to those who had looked after him so well.

Exactly a week later, on 27 March 2020, the Taoiseach made another direct address to the nation, asking everyone to stay at home. Ireland was going into lockdown. We were being asked to restrict how we lived our lives, so that others may live. I had brought Seán home in the nick of time.

Home Home

I hadn't slept properly during the night since Seán was attacked and injured. That's almost two years of tossing and turning and thinking and worrying in those lonely hours of the middle of the night. I felt so alone a lot of the time. Jack, Shauna and Emma tried as much as they could to keep me company. I know all three of them prioritised me over the things that were going on in their own lives to make sure I was okay, skipping nights out with their friends to be with me if I was on my own. But I never wanted them to do that. It was bad enough that they had been through such a worrying time, I just wanted them to be happy. I know that they longed for life to return to normal, but they have always done anything I've asked of them, and more. Their loss has been harder for me to deal with than my own.

They went from having a very carefree normal home life to one that was much more complex. I knew how much they missed the way their dad was before the attack. The fact that they just got on with it and didn't complain nearly made it more emotional for me. I felt a massive sadness over the many milestones Seán had missed: big birthdays like

Emma turning 18 and Jack and Shauna turning 21. Jack's 21st had been spent by Seán's bedside at The Walton Centre in Liverpool. When Shauna's turn came, Seán was in rehab in STEPS in Sheffield and I was living in the UK. I made it home for her party, but she still woke up on the morning of her big birthday with neither of her parents in the country. That was so hard for her, and for me. We had always been the type of family who made a big deal of birthdays, Christmas, anniversaries. Any excuse for a celebration. Jack and Shauna had learned to drive and had passed their tests. As Seán's stay at the NRH in Dún Laoghaire came to an end the previous June, Emma completed her Leaving Cert. Seán had been such a huge help to her with her studies, especially her maths, and I knew she felt his absence massively as she prepared for the exam. Jack and Shauna completed college exams and they all worked hard in their part-time jobs. There were successes on the GAA pitch and in dance competitions. The list goes on.

Seán would have loved being involved in their individual achievements and would have been the first to celebrate their personal wins, and it was very hard for me to accept that the joy of that had been taken away from him, and from them. I know Emma really missed her dad at her debs too. He had been there to celebrate properly with Jack and Shauna. I think she felt really hard done by that it wasn't the same now. As we prepared to get Seán home, Jack was just finishing up his final year in college. He was writing his thesis, something Seán would have had a massive interest and involvement in. He would have loved offering Jack all the support and advice he could, and I know Jack missed that. Even the fact that

Jack was finishing college would have been a huge source of pride for Seán, something to celebrate, and while he knew there was something going on, it was different from the way it would have been before. I think Jack would have also liked his girlfriend, Laura, to have known Seán better before the attack. They had only started going out together right before it happened. Laura has been an incredible support to Jack over the past two years. She could drive before Jack could and used to transport him to visit Seán in whatever hospital he was in at the time. I always felt it was a lot to take on in the very early stages of a relationship, when life should be completely carefree. But their bond just seemed to strengthen as the time went on.

I found it so emotional to watch how each of their individual relationships with Seán had to change. None of them ever complained and any feelings of loss they had were never articulated. It wasn't something we'd ever sit down and discuss. But some things don't need to be voiced and sometimes I could see it in their faces. In the early days when it was touch and go if Seán would even survive, I constantly felt on edge. I could never ever settle. When I'd eventually fall asleep, I'd wake groggy and confused. It would take a few minutes to remember the horror of what had happened, and for a few blissful seconds when I'd open my eyes, I'd have forgotten everything. But then, within a few moments, it would all come flooding back. I'd remember and I'd feel it all over again, like it had just happened. It was exhausting. As the months had gone on, each morning when I'd open my eyes, I'd be struck by Seán's absence in the bed beside me. Sometimes it would take a few seconds to remember where he was. Beaumont Hospital? The National Rehabilitation Hospital? Marymount Nursing Home? Somewhere, but not here. Not at home. And then I'd feel an urge to get up and get to him, wherever he was. My heart just constantly ached to be with Seán. I missed him.

After we finally said our goodbyes to everyone at Marymount Care Centre, me and Jack helped Seán into the car and began our journey home. He knew where he was going. We had driven by the house the day we landed back from Sheffield. He had seen the work that was being carried out. Since then I had spent a lot of time talking to him about the changes we were making to the house. I had shown him videos and photos; one of a digger in our old kitchen which was now his new bedroom. Getting Seán back to the house was something myself and the children had imagined hundreds of times. We had planned a party. We wanted all our family, friends and neighbours to be there to welcome Seán home. We were actually planning on having two parties. But COVID-19 had other plans. We didn't care, though: we had what we wanted. We pulled up outside the house and got Seán into his wheelchair. I wheeled him up the path to our new front door with a feeling in my heart that is too hard to describe. Shauna and Emma were waiting in the garden for us. The look on his face was priceless, he knew exactly where he was. Our neighbours knew Seán was coming home but given the public health guidelines in relation to physical distancing they stayed inside their homes. And in a way it was perfect. It was a moment for just the five of us.

I felt sorry for Seán's brothers and sisters, that they couldn't be there. It was such an important and positive milestone for Seán and for our whole family. Peter, Marty, Sinéad and Suzanne and their families had played such a massive role in helping Seán to get to this point. Over the course of Seán's journey there had been many bad days, days where I struggled to put one foot in front of the other. But knowing we had their support and love really helped me. That evening we sat around our kitchen table and ate dinner together for the first time in almost two years. It was just the five of us, but I knew our close circle were thinking about us. Family and friends had been in touch and I could almost feel the goodwill and warmth of those who couldn't be there in person. My phone beeped with a text from Stephen Felle. He was forwarding a message: 'Stephen, hope you are well. Could you please pass on our best wishes to Seán, Martina and all the family. Fantastically positive news today and hope everything continues in a positive way for the Cox family. All the best, Kenny and Marina Dalglish.' I knew our Liverpool family were also thinking about us. By the time nighttime came around Seán was exhausted. It had been such an emotional day for him, leaving Marymount and getting home. Once he was settled, I went to bed and, for the first time in a long time, I slept like a baby. When I woke up the next morning it felt different, no anxiety and no worry. Seán wasn't there right beside me in the bed but all I had to do to get to him was throw on my dressing gown and walk down the stairs. Finally, I knew where he was. He was home.

Two Years On

I was struggling as we approached the two-year anniversary of Seán's attack. I thought of the old adage of time being a great healer, but I felt like this milestone was dragging me down more than the one-year anniversary had. I knew why. In April 2019 we had been in the thick of our fundraising efforts for Seán's rehab. Plans for the Liverpool Vs Ireland Legends game at the Aviva Stadium were in full swing. There was always something to do, calls to take, meetings to attend. The previous year I had also been in the middle of trying to navigate where Seán would go after the NRH. I used all my spare time researching the best types of rehab and where to access them. Seán was obviously in hospital, so a lot of time was taken up with visiting him and then there were all the different medical appointments too. So, life had been busy and the combination of it all offered me a welcome distraction. But this year, in April 2020 in lockdown Ireland, life was very different.

Our world, like everybody's, had become much smaller and much slower, meaning there was much more time to think. Having Seán at home full time was what we'd been working towards for so long, but it also really highlighted the severity of his injuries and how many challenges he had. I had been warned on that very first day at The Walton Centre in Liverpool that Seán had 'life-changing injuries' and they'd been right. Being with him again 24/7 meant there was no denying that and it was hard and sobering to watch him struggle with the smallest of daily tasks that able-bodied people take for granted. I knew it was important for us not to do everything for Seán. He needed to maintain as much independence as he could, so we encouraged him to do certain things for himself. He needed plenty of time and things could get messy but if we'd learned one thing over the past two years it was how to be patient. We went at his pace, and being in lockdown gave us all the time in the world to do so. I knew what I wanted our new normal to look like. Leaving STEPS in Sheffield I had wished I could bottle everything about the place – the atmosphere, the ethos, the positivity. I wanted to mirror that at home. I planned a full programme of therapies to keep Seán busy during the week: physiotherapy, speech, language and music therapy. When I was drawing up his schedule, I also made sure Seán had time to rest in between each session. I had seen the importance of that first-hand at STEPS. Even if he didn't want to sleep, I was going to make sure he went into his room for some quiet time before he'd start work again. But the COVID-19 restrictions knocked this plan off course.

Because of the physical distancing guidelines, his physiotherapy was stopped. We continued with his speech therapy through Zoom, which he actually took to really well which surprised us. We did what we had always done as a family – we tried to fill the gaps and do as much as we could to keep Seán engaged and stimulated. The safest thing was to keep ourselves to ourselves. Seán was vulnerable. If he got the virus it could have serious implications for him. We couldn't take any risks so we followed the public health advice as much as we could. But Seán's carers had to come to the house every day to help me look after him. I was terrified they might bring the virus into the house but without them it wasn't possible to have Seán at home. There was no way around it. The only thing we could do was make sure we were following all the guidelines around hygiene. We took every precaution we could and hoped for the best. Sharing our house with Seán's team of carers was a real adjustment for all of us. When we were preparing to get Seán home I used to try to imagine what it was going to be like, to have people I didn't know moving around our house. But it's one of those things you can't really conjure up until you're actually experiencing it first-hand. Apart from a few hours in the afternoon, Seán has a carer with him at all times. They are lifesavers but at the beginning it felt like we had a bunch of strangers living under our roof. Sometimes at night I'd hear movement downstairs and get a fright, and then I'd remember that it wasn't just the five of us in the house anymore.

Seán also found parts of it hard to deal with, especially the personal care elements. I did whatever I could to keep him positive and upbeat, reminding him he'd be showered and back in his chair in no time at all. Jack, Shauna and Emma also struggled with having people we didn't know living with us. I think at first they felt they had to act differently, be quieter or careful about what they said or did, like the house wasn't their own space anymore. But slowly as the weeks went on we all got used to one another – the faces, the names, the personalities. It was our new way of living. Sounds that had once been strange took on their own familiarity. I made sure I spent time getting to know the carers, building up a relationship with them. I knew if Seán saw me getting on with them, he would take his lead from me. I wanted him to be able to trust them. It was a steep learning curve for all of us.

Every day the carers got to know more about Seán. Was he a morning person? Did he take sugar in his coffee? 'Dad prefers those biscuits,' Emma would remind them. We made sure they knew what he liked and didn't like. Even though we now had him home I still felt that urge to speak up for him. Imagine wanting or needing something and not being able to communicate it? That broke my heart. We also learned a lot from the carers, the way they made Seán comfortable in bed, how they moved him into his chair with such ease. At the start I thought I'd never be able to get Seán up from his bed and into his chair. I was afraid I'd let him fall. Jack mastered the technique with ease. 'He's not a doll,' he'd say, all business, as he'd help him onto the standing turner and into his chair. Now it's something I do without even thinking about it.

As 24 April rolled around, distractions from thinking about how events had unfolded two years before were thin on the ground and I was worried about how we'd pass the day. It was a Friday, takeaway night in our house. The day before I headed to the supermarket to pick up a few bits.

On my way back I checked the post box. As I opened one of the letters a business card fell out. It belonged to a journalist called Conor Feehan who works for Independent News and Media. Immediately I felt uneasy. This could only mean bad news. He began his letter by explaining that he had been covering Seán's story since the attack and had travelled to Liverpool the day after it had happened, and that he was glad to see that Seán was now home. He went on, 'I am conscious of the fact that tomorrow will be the second anniversary of the attack on Seán and with that in mind I made a query to the Ministry of Justice in the UK to establish where the three Italian men who were convicted surrounding the attack are.' I held my breath and continued to read. 'I was somewhat surprised to learn they have all been released, although the dates they left prison is information that I do not have.' No, this couldn't be true. He must have it wrong, I thought to myself. I read on. 'It's likely you know this information already but on the off chance that you do not I thought it would be fair to you to let you know that I will be including that fact in a piece I am writing for tomorrow's paper so that you would know about it in advance.'

I didn't know this information and I really couldn't believe what I was reading. It was just over a year ago that we had been in Preston for the trial of Simone Mastrelli. He had been sentenced to three and a half years in prison. That was only 14 months ago – surely he was still in prison? I was devastated. I had always felt the sentences that were handed down to the three Italian men did not represent justice for Seán, but to think that they had been released before they had even completed those sentences was too much. All three of them had spent less time in prison than Seán had spent in hospital over the past two years. Where is the fairness in that? Getting that news made the second anniversary very difficult for all of us. We were all angry and upset but we couldn't show it. Seán was at home now with us and we had to keep the show on the road.

I had to break the news to Seán's family. Marty was particularly floored. He was the only one of us who had witnessed first-hand the brutality and viciousness of the attack. I know Marty will live with what happened that day in Anfield for the rest of his life. He still finds it hard to get past the fact that if he hadn't been given the tickets for the match, Seán wouldn't have been there that day. The chances of being at the match in the first place were so slim; the chances of them being in that exact spot on Walton Breck Road at that wrong moment were even slimmer. What if he had been standing on Seán's right-hand side? Would he have taken the blow to the side of the head instead? I know those questions still torment him, and probably always will. He was personally hurt by the news that the three Italian men had been released early. Seán had in many ways been given a life sentence yet those responsible could now get back to living their lives as if nothing had ever happened. They had gotten away scot-free and no lessons had been learned. Would they do it again? I later received a call from Detective Inspector Paul Speight from Merseyside Police. He had not been made aware of the development and was as surprised as I was. DI Speight and his team had worked fast and hard to arrest the three men and a huge amount of time had gone into putting the case together. But after that it was out of their hands. I have always tried so hard to not let the anger get in on me. I made that decision very early on. It just wasn't an option for me. I knew it wouldn't serve me or my family well.

That evening as we sat down to dinner I felt so upset. Seán had done nothing wrong. He was an innocent bystander who got caught in an act of mindless violence. And now he had to live with so many disabilities. I was finding it hard not to feel bitter about it all, but in moments like that Jack, Shauna and Emma always pulled me back. I know they sometimes ask themselves, 'Why us? Why did this have to happen to Seán and our family?' but all three of them chose to look forward and not back. And I learn from them every day. Jack once told me that he had heard someone ask if it would have been better if Seán had not survived the attack. He was so badly injured; would it have been easier if he had died? His answer stopped me in my tracks. 'I'd rather have the new version of Dad here than no dad at all.' I watch them pull themselves together because they know things could be a whole lot worse. They also know if they're happy, Seán is happy. And he is. He might not be able to tell us but when he's surrounded by his family at home his smile tells us everything we need to know.

Our New Normal

As the halfway point of 2020 arrived it really felt like COVID-19 had changed the world. Life had been altered by a virus that no one had heard of six months earlier. The virus had a devastating impact on nursing homes, including Marymount Care Centre. I was heartbroken when I heard the news that 28 residents at the nursing home had passed away after contracting COVID-19. I felt so sad for the families who had lost a loved one, and for the McNultys. I had seen with my own eyes the love they had for their residents and the standard of care that was consistently delivered. Seán had been so well looked after there. I thought back to the day I was first told that visiting was being restricted. Management had been so determined to make sure they kept the virus out of the nursing home. Many of Marymount's residents had been with them for years; they were going to do whatever they could to protect them. Every day I was thankful I had managed to get Seán home before the nursing home went into lockdown. But I felt a deep sadness for everyone involved and just couldn't imagine what they were going through.

Everyone talked about finding a 'new normal', but I think we had already found ours. As each day passed Seán became more settled at home. In a way, we all had to learn to live together again. Seán had to get used to the hustle and bustle of us all being in a room together. When Seán was in hospital Jack, Shauna and Emma mostly visited him at different times. We never really wanted to leave him on his own for long, so it was a better use of resources for them to visit on different evenings. This meant that Seán hadn't really been surrounded by all three of his children for two years except when we had gathered together for special occasions. I knew it was going to be strange at first for Seán to have so many of us in the one place. I'd always been hell-bent on making sure he got all the stimulation he needed but we had to be careful to take it at his pace. All four of us talking at him at the one time was going to be too much for him so I knew we'd have to find a new rhythm that we'd all be comfortable with. It was important that we communicated with Seán in a clear and concise way to give him the best chance of understanding us.

More words started to come to Seán and being around us really helped. We managed to draw him into conversation in a very natural and organic way. He still can't initiate a chat but he's aware of everything that's going on around him. If the two girls are fighting over something, he'll look at me as if to say, 'Here we go again.' He is working hard at his speech and therapy and he will talk if we prompt him, which we do constantly. 'Yeah' is still his default word but we push him to say other things. If I say to him, 'Tea or coffee?' he might say, 'Yeah', but I keep going until he decides and tells me which one he'd actually prefer. He also managed to add the word 'virus' to his vocabulary. I had to try to explain what was going on with all the restrictions and why people couldn't come to visit him. It was so hard on his family. His brothers and sisters had been so committed to him over the previous two years. They had spent countless hours at his bedside in different hospitals willing him along the road to recovery. After a day's work they'd arrive to spend their evenings with him. And it was hard, especially in the early days when he was still very sleepy. Seán's sister Suzanne had gone on to marry 'Seán from Galway' who she had met in those early years when we worked in Dunnes Stores in Kilnamanagh. Around the time myself and Seán moved to Dunboyne they moved to Galway, so she was that bit further away from us. But she always made a huge effort to come to Dublin to see Seán as did Marty, who was working in Dublin but living in Laois. They had never ever let him down. And now he was home, and they had to stay away.

The 'Seán's Recovery' WhatsApp group was still going strong so I made sure to send lots of photos and videos of Seán settling in at home until the group could get to see him properly. I knew this would keep them going until we could all be reunited again. Seán found it strange too as he was so used to seeing them. One of the days during lockdown his sister arrived at the door to drop in a birthday card for Jack. Seán saw her from the window and his face lit up but she couldn't come in. He looked so disappointed so I asked him, 'You know why Sinéad can't come in?' He replied, 'Virus'. It wasn't one of the words I had expected to be in Seán's very limited vocabulary. Even though our family life had changed so much, Jack, Shauna and Emma continued to treat Seán like their dad. I know Emma found it hard to tell people about Seán when she started college and began to make new friends. Coming out with, 'My dad has a brain injury,' is a bit of a conversation killer but it is such a big part of our lives it's hard when people don't know. Most people do know and are very familiar with Seán's story. This has been a challenge, too.

Shauna in particular has always been really uncomfortable with Seán's story being a very public one. 'We're just an ordinary family from Dunboyne, we didn't ask for any of this,' she'd say over and over again. She knew why it was important for us to talk about him and thank people for all the help they had given us, but she never liked the spotlight being on our family. I remember she was sitting on a beach in Thailand in 2019 when an Irish guy her group had met up with asked her was she Seán Cox's daughter. She couldn't believe it. They all found their own way of being with Seán. Shauna has a particularly unique way with her dad. She is studying Early Childhood Studies in Marino Institute of Education in Dublin so is probably the most equipped to help him. Over the past two years she has learned a lot about how best to communicate with people, how to be patient and the best way to teach different skills. Herself and Seán have always pushed each other's buttons and it's no different now. When he sees Shauna coming in to him, he gives me a 'here she comes' look. Shauna pushes him to learn new skills like throwing and catching a ball in the garden or writing his name. She works hard with him but, most importantly, she still makes him laugh. She knows that if he's happy and enjoying a certain task, he'll stay engaged with it for longer. It's incredible to watch them together like that. But the best thing all three of them can give their dad is time and they do this in spades. They sit with him for hours and include him in every little thing that's going on in their lives.

The COVID-19 restrictions had a massive impact on all live sport, which was hard for Seán. The Premier League had been suspended, with Liverpool just two wins away from the title, and no one knew if it would resume. Seán really missed it. Despite everything he has been through, the enjoyment he gets from watching sport never waned. I never thought I'd be someone who would wish for the return of football, but I was. Jack played a big role here. He kept him abreast of everything that was going on, he found old matches and tournaments for Seán to watch and picked out box sets he knew he would enjoy. He also kept him up to date on the comings and goings at St Peter's GAA Club. Before the attack, Seán and Jack were always at their happiest watching their beloved Liverpool play a match with a cold beer. They'd take to their man cave to watch and you could hear the shouting and roaring right around the house. Even our two dogs, Roxy and Bruno, would run for cover. Thankfully, that hasn't changed. Seán used to love a pint of Guinness, but he doesn't like it from a can. Jack couldn't wait to wheel him down to our local, Slevin's, for a proper pint when the pubs opened again.

Emma sometimes second-guesses herself with Seán, wondering if she is doing the right thing, feeling a little inferior to Shauna. But she has the most loving and caring nature with her dad. She is the one to make sure Seán is never in pain and always comfortable. She is his baby. One day I walked into Seán's room to find him with tears running down his face. 'On no, what's wrong?' I asked. He pointed at the television. He'd been watching a rerun of the 2010 Masters in Augusta. The champion, Phil Mickelson, was talking about his wife, Amy, who had been diagnosed with breast cancer the previous year. Mickelson had taken a break from golf to look after her but had won the Masters on his return. Amy's health had improved and Mickelson was speaking about how brilliant it was to have her there that day to share in a very special moment after a really tough year. I thought back to a time in the early days when I wondered would Seán feel things the way he used to. I guess I had my answer. Personally, for me the hardest part of lockdown was not who I couldn't see, but who I could. I only really left the house to go grocery shopping, but every time I did, I saw couples heading off for a walk or a run together. A lot of people were either out of work or working from home and I think most people tried to exercise, just for something to do. Seeing those couples chatting and laughing together as they walked or jogged along made me miss Seán so much. I would have done anything to be able to do something so simple with Seán again. In fact, I knew if the COVID-19 lockdown had happened before Seán was attacked, he would have run the legs off me getting out of the house for our daily allotted exercise.

I missed the most mundane, ordinary things the most. On the bad days I felt that loss very deeply. I also felt the loss of some people who used to be in our lives who disappeared after Seán was attacked. Most people had gone beyond all expectations to help us, and I knew I would never be able to properly thank them for all they had done. But there were others who I think just couldn't deal with what had happened to Seán: maybe they didn't know what to say or what to do. Seán being different made some people feel uncomfortable. It is different now but me and Seán are still the same couple. We can't do the things we used to be able to do, not without a lot of planning and preparation. At times it felt like we had fallen off people's radars. Out of sight, out of mind. I think there's still a lot of mystery and intrigue around brain injuries and, in many ways, I understand that. It's a complex condition. If what happened to Seán hadn't happened, I wouldn't know what I know now. Unfortunately, in Ireland you must navigate your own journey; it's not straightforward and can often result in a dead end. People must find the answers themselves and make their own plans. I knew Seán wouldn't be the last Irish person to suffer a brain injury, but I hoped that in time the path to recovery would become clearer. Some days what happened hit me like a ton of bricks.

One day on my way back from my weekly escape to the supermarket I passed a sign at the entrance to our housing estate advertising the redevelopment of St Peter's GAA Club. I felt like crying. Seán had such a deep love for the club. His link with the place was what had initially given us such a sense of belonging and community when we had first come to Dunboyne. If what happened hadn't happened, he no doubt would have been front and centre in whatever it was that was going on. And yet he didn't even know it was happening. So much had been taken away from him, and from us.

June 2020 saw a slight easing of the COVID-19 restrictions and on Monday 15 June, I emerged from lockdown to return to work at Dunnes Stores. My alarm woke me at 6 a.m. I was nervous but excited to get back. I had kept in contact with Anne Heffernan over the previous months. 'When you're ready, come back, but only when you're ready,' she said. I arranged my hours to make sure I was back in the early afternoon to take care of Seán. I got myself ready and made my way downstairs to have a chat with Seán's carer before I left. When I was ready to go, I looked in on him, sleeping peacefully in his bed. I felt a tug on my heartstrings about leaving him. Like most people during lockdown we had spent all day, every day together. It reminded me of how I had felt many years before on my return to work from maternity leave on Jack, Shauna and Emma. It was always so hard to go back after living in that newborn bubble. Those three babies were now all young adults who could thankfully fend for themselves. But I was worried about Seán. Would he miss me? Would he wonder where I had gone and not be able to ask? 'Call me if you need anything,' I reminded the carer as I left the house. 'Everything will be fine,' I told myself as I drove away.

I was going back to the homewares department and was again based in head office on George's Street in Dublin city centre. The restrictions in place to stop the spread of COVID-19 and the guidelines around physical distancing meant the office was half empty as lots of people were still working from home. Nevertheless, it was great to be reunited with people that I hadn't seen in a long time. Everyone was so interested to hear how Seán was doing. Most people knew he had come home but they all wanted to know how he had settled in. I lost count of the amount of times I was asked, 'How's Seán?' Before long it felt like I had never been away. I really enjoy the whole process involved in being a buyer, picking a range that will ultimately end up on the shelves in stores around the country. I always felt very lucky and privileged to have a job that really interests me. I'd get so immersed in what I was doing it was hard to think about anything else and at times that was exactly what I needed. I had been so consumed by everything to do with Seán and how I could help him as best as I could over the past two years, I really hadn't thought about anything else. Going out to work meant I had to park all my worries for a certain amount of time each day, which I think was really good for my mental health. It was also good for Seán as it gave him a bit more independence. I had always worked, so it was our normal. Our new normal. It was so nice to be reunited with Seán when my day was over, and I think he felt the same. When I arrived home from my second day back in work, Seán's carer and Emma told me he had been a bit grumpy. But when I walked into his room his face lit up as he welcomed me with the biggest smile.

To the Future

For many people, 2020 will probably be remembered as the year the world was turned upside-down. And for so many people it was. But we'll remember it very differently. For us the world was suddenly the right way around. We had Seán back home. It forced us to stop and just be together as a family, something we hadn't done in two years. If things had been different, I would have been back in work sooner and Jack, Shauna and Emma would have been in college, working part time and living their lives. Being asked to stay at home was a blessing for us as a family. It gave us time to make some plans, to contemplate the future. For so long we had been afraid to do that and had existed in the moment because that was all we had. We were guaranteed nothing. Having Seán back home with us and feeling well was all we had wished for over the past two years. We took advantage of the beautiful weather we had been blessed with. On one of the sunny days I wheeled Seán out into our back garden. I placed him under the shade but he waved his hand at me and pointed to a sunnier spot. I laughed as I moved him over to sit beside me. 'Seán's face is a bit red, is he sunburnt?' his carer asked me that night. 'Oh, he'll be okay,' I replied as I rubbed a bit of aftersun into his cheeks. After spending more than two years in hospital, sitting out and enjoying a bit of the glorious sunshine was the best thing for him. I felt blessed he was here to do it.

We celebrated Jack and Emma's birthdays. As Jack turned 23 we thought back on his 21st, which we'd spent at Seán's bedside in intensive care in Liverpool before going to Nando's for dinner. We really had come a long way since then. It felt like it was time to start living life again. I arranged a nice birthday brunch with all Jack's favourite food to celebrate. It was just so lovely to be together. None of us cared that we had to stay at home and that we couldn't do anything more extravagant. It was perfect. The sun was shining for Emma's birthday too. We ordered a takeaway to eat in the garden. 'Pass the garlic bread, please,' Emma asked no one in particular as we all tucked into our meal. We were all too busy stuffing our faces, so no one heard her. 'Pass the garlic bread, PLEASE,' she asked again. Without missing a beat Seán lifted his hand, grabbed the garlic bread and placed it in front of Emma. It took us all by surprise. Realistically Seán will never walk again but with the right help he will get stronger. But he's certainly aware of everything that's going on around him. After Emma blew out her birthday candles, the conversation turned to Portugal. We'd all been thinking about it but were afraid to say it. We wanted to go back. I know Seán would hate us to stop living our lives because of the attack. What happened outside Anfield stadium on 24 April 2018 had shaped all our lives but it didn't have to define them. We agreed it was possible once one of Seán's carers came with us. At least I knew he wouldn't get burnt! We added it to the bucket list.

By the middle of June Ireland's roadmap back to normality had been accelerated and Seán could see his brothers and sisters again. We could all be reunited. In another address to the nation Leo Varadkar said, 'We have all been through a shared experience and as we move forward we will never forget what we have lost, what we have learned and what we have gained.' I couldn't have put it better myself. June also saw the much welcome return of live football. On Wednesday 24 June 2020 Seán watched Liverpool take on Crystal Palace at Anfield. It felt surreal with no crowds in the stadium, but the excitement and anticipation was still there. He cheered every goal as his beloved team moved ever closer to the Premier League title with a 4–0 win. The club's 30-year wait was almost over. The last time they had done it, Seán was in his twenties. He had cheered them on and celebrated with his brothers in his mam's house. It was only a year after his dad had passed away. Now they were on the cusp of doing it again – it was a matter of when and not if. The following day I got out the 'Seán Cox' banner the Liverpool players had paraded around the Stadio Olimpico in Rome a few days after Seán was attacked. I put it over his bed and tucked him in. He was ready. The next evening Chelsea beat Manchester City 2–1, a win that meant Liverpool were crowned the champions of England for the first time since 1990. Liverpool CEO Peter Moore tweeted, 'Number 19 is finally here. It's for our millions of fans, near and far … we miss you. It's for the Reds that fell to the virus. It's for my dad who first took me to Anfield in 1959. It's for Seán Cox, smiling in Ireland right now. And it's for the 96, who will never be forgotten.'

Since the attack people have often admired my strength and commitment to Seán, but I've never seen it like that. I only did what anyone would do for the man they loved. Seán had fought so hard to get better, to stay with us. I was just walking the road with him. In many ways he had defied all the odds. He had recovered in ways no one thought he would. That Saturday morning, I woke up early, put on my dressing gown and made my way downstairs to Seán's bedroom. Seán works hard at all his different therapies during the week, so I like to make the weekends a bit different for him. It's nice for him to know there's no 'work' today. His carer got him up and into his chair. 'Good morning,' I said as I entered his bedroom. He gave me a thumbs-up and a beautiful smile. His bed looked so cosy, so I jumped in. It was still warm from him. As I lay there, my mind travelled back over all the times it was Seán lying in the bed, and me sitting beside him. I thought about all the wishes I had made. 'Please, please, survive the night,' I prayed at the beginning. 'Open your eyes, Seán, please know who I am.' As time went on I wished for more: 'Give me a smile, Seán, talk to me, let me hear your voice again.' Lost in thought, my eyes felt heavy. As they closed, Seán grabbed my hand. 'There he is,' I thought to myself. Once we have each other nothing else matters.

Acknowledgements

eán, this book is dedicated to you, for all you have been through. It's been some journey. You have come a long way from the very early days in the Walton Centre when we really weren't sure if you'd pull through, but you're here with us even though life has changed dramatically. We may not be able to communicate the way we used to, but the love and the bond we have is as strong as ever.

To Jack, Shauna and Emma. Life has not been easy since Dad's attack, but I could not be prouder of the way you all have dealt with this awful situation. Dad may not be able to express in words how he is feeling, but the smile on his face when you are around speaks volumes. Here's to our new normal, all back together as a family and embracing life to the full.

To Suzanne, Peter, Martin, Sinéad and the extended Cox family. Thank you for your unwavering support. It's been very tough going at times, but the love and support you have shown Seán, myself and the kids has made it more bearable. We look forward to many family gatherings in Dunboyne.

To my dad, my sisters, Bernie and Catherine, and brothers, Patrick and Terence. Thanks for being there for me and the kids in so many ways – we truly appreciate all you have done. Christmas morning is in our home this year!

To Seán's cousin, Richard, and his wife, Una, who have been a constant support in so many ways.

To Susan Keogh, my ghostwriter. We had only met once before we started the book, but I knew we had connected. Thank you for the endless hours we spent chatting during lockdown, for getting inside my head and somehow expressing the words in a way that I felt so comfortable with. You really believed in bringing the story to life and have done so in such a powerful way.

Thanks to all the ladies in Gill Books who helped me along the way.

To my friends, some of whom I mention in the book and others I do not. I am forever grateful for the constant support, endless cups of coffee and lunches, and just a listening ear when I needed it. To the friends whom I had lost touch with but have since been reacquainted with over the last two years, that has meant a lot to me. To my running buddies for getting me out on the track: the head space and company has been great. To my Portugal pals: we don't see each other a lot, but we will be forever connected.

To my neighbours, who helped so much when I was in the Walton Centre with Seán and looked out for the kids.

To Stacey Looby, a community guard, for all her fundraising and thoughtfulness. And to Becky and Ricenda Ward, Shauna and Emma's dance teachers, for supporting and encouraging them.

WITH HOPE IN YOUR HEART

To all of Seán's therapists, who come to our home to help Seán in his recovery by steadily pushing and encouraging him. To Seán's team of carers, who look after him so well. A big thank you to everyone.

To those who have cared for Seán to support his recovery over the past number of years, including the Walton Centre, Beaumont Hospital, the National Rehabilitation Hospital, STEPS, and the wonderful staff at Marymount Care Centre.

To Stephen Felle and Fergus McNulty, who took me under their wing. I was at a very low point with the realisation of the extent of Seán's life-changing injuries and knew there would be a need to fundraise to ensure that Seán was going to get the best possible chance. The Seán Cox Rehabilitation Trust was established to administer the monies raised and pay for Seán's long-term care. My thanks to the trustees, Stephen Felle, David Gantly, Kevin McKeown, Paul Noonan and treasurer Billy Jones, for the advice and time they have given Seán and me.

To Mick O'Keeffe and his wonderful team at Teneo, who handled media for me and the family from early on, as well as the PR around all of the fundraising events for Seán. The events are almost too many to list and to remember, but several stand out for acknowledgement.

To the organisers of the Meath Vs Dublin GAA match in Páirc Tailteann in December 2018: Fergus McNulty, Jim Gavin, Andy McEntee, as well as all the players who took part to make this a memorable occasion.

For the Run for Seán in October of that year, my appreciation must go to Teresa Smith, Noel Leddy, Keith Eglington and all at Dunboyne Athletics Club. Also the 2019

Dublin Night Run for which Seán was the chosen charity, and the Sixes for Seán soccer tournament run by Brian Conway and Carol Pearl at Ratoath Harps AFC.

To the Legends for Seán Cox committee, which was formed to organise the Ireland XI Vs Liverpool Legends in the Aviva Stadium and the gala dinner in the Intercontinental Hotel events in April 2019. A busy group of business and sports people, most of whom had no connection with Seán, gave so much in making those events huge successes: Brendan Quinn, Colm Duggan, Darragh Maloney, David Gantly, Denis O'Brien, Emmet Kavanagh, Fergus McNulty, John Delaney, Kevin McKeown, Michael O'Flynn, Mick O'Keeffe, Noel Keeley, Pat Cooney, Paul Noonan, Peter Moore, Seán Mulryan, Sinead Spain, Stephen Cooney, Stephen Daly, Stephen Felle and Tommy Lyons. To the retired stars of Ireland and Liverpool FC who played in the Aviva that day under the management of Mick McCarthy and Kenny Dalglish. To Cathal Dervan and his team at the FAI, Michael Murphy of the Aviva Stadium, the dinner organiser Paul Byrnes, and everyone else who made them such momentous events for Seán, me and the family.

To everyone who put such enormous effort into filling the 3Arena for the John Bishop and Friends comedy extravaganza in January 2020. To all the comedians – John Bishop, Michael McIntyre, Dara Ó Briain, Deirdre O'Kane, Des Bishop, Jason Byrne, Joanne McNally and Tommy Tiernan – who gave so generously of their time and made Seán laugh and laugh. To John's producer, Adam Scott, and to Bren Berry, Peter Aiken, Mary Kelly and all of the wonderful people at Aiken Promotions and the 3Arena.

To Fergus O'Callaghan, the O'Sullivan family and all of Seán's great friends and supporters across the electrical industry for their fundraising efforts in aid of Seán.

I need to thank the executive and entire membership of St Peter's GAA Club in Dunboyne and the village of Dunboyne, who were the engine room for supporting the various fundraising efforts for Seán, in particular Stephen Felle, Fergus McNulty, Andrea and Gus Lynch, Gillian Reilly, Brian Howlin, Derick Murphy, Billy Jones, Ciara and Brendan Quinn, Lenny Rooney, Ronan O'Doherty, Linda Kane and Martin Craig. My gratitude, too, to The Dunboyne Collective, a group of singers and children from our village who came together to record a special version of 'You'll Never Walk Alone' for Seán. The whole parish of Dunboyne have been an invaluable source of solidarity and support for us as a family. I never really knew the true meaning of community until Seán's attack, and we feel incredibly lucky to be part of it.

To all associated with the renovation of our house, which has allowed Seán to return home to us, including Gary Mongey, Kevin Casey, Will McLoughlin, Ronan O'Sullivan, Damian Curley, Matt Dwyer, Niall McNulty, Richard Smith, Declan and Claire Mahon, Chadwicks in Lucan, Diarmuid Gavin and Paul Smith.

To my colleagues at Dunnes Stores, Margaret and Ann Heffernan, and the entire Dunne family for their support and understanding. You all made things easier for Seán over the past few years in many ways, for which I will be forever grateful.

To the people I have gotten to know over the past two years who have become part of my fight for Seán, and who have quietly helped us in so many ways, including Claire Byrne, Eugene Larkin, Sinead Spain, Dudley Sloan, Stephen Jones, Michael O'Flynn, Darragh Maloney, Peter and Debbie Moore, Emmet Kavanagh, Seamus Coleman, John Greene, Jennifer O'Connell, Martin Phelan, Brian Duffy, Damien O'Reilly, Maria Murphy and many more I know I have forgotten to name here, but to whom I owe so much!

To Liverpool Football Club. I didn't get the 'We are Liverpool, We are Family' slogan until Seán's attack, but I do now. Thanks to Peter Moore, Susan Black, Matt McCann and Billy Hogan at executive level; Jürgen Klopp and his players, who remain Seán's idols; Jen Carter, Tony Barrett, David Evans, Tina Roberts and everyone in the club who has helped us at various stages; and to past players, including Jamie Carragher, Ian Rush, Jason McAteer and Robbie Fowler, who have been extremely generous in their support for Seán.

My appreciation to Stephen 'Mono' Monaghan and all at the Spirit of Shankly supporters club, who very much saw Seán as one of their own and have never forgotten his plight.

When I decided to write this book, I hoped that it would help me in some way to come to terms with Seán's dreadful attack. The endless hours talking through my story with Susan Keogh, my ghostwriter, has definitely helped me through this and I hope that my story might help other families going through similar situations.

Go with your gut instinct and do what you feel is best for your loved one. There is always hope.

Martina

—⟨∞⟩—

Writing this book with Martina has been the ultimate privilege for me. As a journalist, I've been familiar with Seán's story since the attack in 2018, but Martina's resilience in dealing with how their life has changed has completely blown me away. Martina poured her heart and soul into this book and I laughed and cried along the way.

Taking this project on during a global pandemic, while working full time and with schools off, was at times a challenge. I could not have done it without my husband, Stephen, and my daughter, Faith. They kept the show on the road at home and never doubted I could do it, even when I doubted myself. To my mam and dad, Jane, Conor, Declan and Laura for their constant support of everything I do: thank you. And to my close friends, who never forgot to check in on me. You know who you are.

To my former boss, Communicorp's Head of News Sinead Spain, I will never be able to thank you for the hours you've lost listening to how this story evolved. You were the first person I ever told I wanted to write this book, and you've been cheering me on ever since. I will be forever grateful that you pushed me to do it, and for your support and friendship.

Thank you to everyone at Gill Books: Catherine Gough, Sarah Liddy, Teresa Daly and Ellen Monnelly, a team of tremendous women.

To Liverpool Football Club, especially Manager Jürgen Klopp, former CEO Peter Moore and Communications Director Susan Black. Thank you for being so generous with your time during what was a very busy period for the club. And to Seán and Martina's friends, Fergus McNulty and Stephen Felle, for their input.

To Seán's brother Marty Cox, who was with Seán in Anfield on 24 April 2018. Thank you for reliving the nightmare with such clarity and honesty. I know how hard it was for you, and I hope our chat and the book helps in some way.

To Jack, Shauna and Emma. What can I say? I'm still thinking about how incredible you three are. Trust me when I say anyone who has ever had children could only hope they turn out like you guys. I know how proud your mam and dad are of you.

COVID-19 restrictions eased as we came to the end of this project, which meant I could finally travel to Dunboyne to spend some time with Martina and Seán. Their house is one of the most peaceful environments I've ever been in. The love between the two of them was what attracted me to this story in the first instance, but even I was taken aback when I witnessed them together. The way they communicate, the way they laugh, the way they look at one another. It really is a sight to behold.

I felt a massive responsibility to do this story justice for the Cox family, but also for anyone who has ever had the rug pulled from underneath them when they least expected it. This story is extremely valuable. It shows how hope can be found in heartbreak if you try hard enough. Thank you, Martina, for sharing your story with me. I know you'll roll your eyes at this, but I have learned so much along the way. Lessons I will take with me and treasure. You are a powerhouse. People will remember lockdown for many different reasons, but for me it will always be the time I made a friend for life.

Susan